ANTIQUES
ACROSS AMERICA

ANTIQUES
ACROSS AMERICA

NANCY McCARTHY

The CONFIDENT COLLECTOR™

AVON BOOKS ◆ NEW YORK

Information contained herein is subject to change without notice. Every effort has been made to provide the most accurate information available at the time of publication. Avon Books assumes no responsibility for any difficulty resulting from a change in information.

AVON BOOKS
A division of
The Hearst Corporation
1350 Avenue of the Americas
New York, New York 10019

For my son
David
whose help and encouragement
made this book possible

CONTENTS

CONTENTS

INTRODUCTION

Many dealers end up in the antiques business accidentally. All of a sudden, they realize they've been to one yard sale too many, and the fantastic treasures they've been dragging home triumphantly every weekend have reached some sort of critical mass state. Now there is no choice. If they ever want to buy anything again, they have to unload.

That's essentially what happened to me, although I went on to take the next truly foolhardy step and started an antique co-op in the Hamptons on New York's Long Island. Suddenly I had an actual business going and before too long it was successful enough so that I was able to move out west to live out my lifelong western fantasy. That included my own antique shop in the ski resort of Steamboat Springs, Colorado.

I have to tell you—it was great! Shooting around Steamboat Springs in my pickup truck (mandatory for a westerner) early on Saturday mornings to check out yard sales for a few hours before I opened the store, with all these incredible mountain vistas and beautiful horses around and hot air balloons floating overhead, was an almost mystical experience. There are a lot of people around who will tell you that all the magic and a lot of the fun have gone out of the antiques business because all the real goodies have been discovered. That's not true in Steamboat Springs or in almost every other part of the country I've explored.

What has happened is an explosion of interest in collecting, so dealers now have a lot more competition. But the fantastic buys definitely are still out there.

A few months ago, I found a Revolutionary War era leather-covered travel trunk in such pristine condition it could be in a museum. I bought it from another dealer for $75. That's the attraction, the lure that has hooked so many of us. Where else are you going to find something aesthetically pleasing, rich in history, and worth more than you paid for it? It's very easy to become addicted to the excitement of the hunt.

It was quite a while before I came to my senses and all that time—I'm a slow learner so it took about ten years—I often felt as though I specialized in learning everything the hard way, making the types of mistakes in buying and selling antiques that imprinted themselves permanently in your brain because you feel so stupid when you find out what you've done wrong this time.

One of the first pieces of furniture I stripped was a washstand with a coat of green enamel on it that was so ugly it made me wish there were paint police. It was easy enough to remove, but underneath the green was a stubborn, dark red paint that wouldn't budge. I finally wound up sanding the red off, but it never did come out completely and the washstand had a sort of rosy glow that stayed in the wood. It was quite a while before I found out that the stubborn red stuff was the original milk-paint finish and of course I'd completely ruined the value of the washstand by taking it off.

And then there's the nineteenth-century Pembroke table I cut down to coffee-table size because I didn't know what it was, with essentially the same result: value gone. Or, there was the Georgia face jug I sold for four dollars after paying only fifty cents for it at a yard sale; the face on the round earthenware jug was so ugly it make me uncomfortable and really anxious to get rid of it. My margin of profit seemed just fine until I learned the real value of that jug—$125, and that was a while ago.

Well, anyway, while making all those mistakes I was picking up knowledge, too, and getting it from the best possible sources—other people who were experts or at least had more experience.

INTRODUCTION

Steamboat Springs was a great place to collect
good advice; it attracted people from all over the
country for skiing in the winter and mountain vaca-
tions in the summer. Because there's nothing antiques enthusiasts like better than talking about their
great finds after they've checked out a store, dealers
who stopped in would tell me where they'd made
some of their most fantastic discoveries. Most of
these places were in other states far away, so they
didn't mind sharing their secrets with me because I
wasn't ever going to be competition.

The ardent collectors were even more fun to talk
to. They'd fill me in on all the arcane elements involved in whatever it was they'd be trying to find,
so on any given afternoon I might be learning how
to tell the difference between a garden-variety old
bike and a prized Schwinn worth a couple thousand
dollars, or finding out that the official length of a
piece of barbed wire has to be at least eighteen
inches or it doesn't count.

Did you know that barbed wire collectors have
their own convention every year? And a price guide?
I learned all that from a very charming elderly gen-
tleman who started his barbed wire collection with
a two-hundred-foot roll he bought impulsively for
$20 at an auction. He told me he'd cut it into eighteen-
inch lengths, sold each one for $5 or $10 and made
more than $1,000, enough to make a good start on
what became an award-winning collection.

Armed with esoteric information like that, I

xiv

started to travel in the off seasons, looking for some of the places visiting dealers had been telling me about—the shops, malls, flea markets, and auctions where they found the merchandise they bought to stock their stores.

And while I was exploring the country, figuring out where the best bargains were hidden, I was learning how to shop as well. It really is better to know what you're doing when you're hot on the trail of the great buy. If you want to pay dealer prices, you have to learn to shop the same way the dealers do.

In this book you're going to learn about a lot of places that dealers would never even whisper about if a customer were within earshot. Very few of these places advertise and often you won't read about most of them in tourist guides.

Some of them are one-owner shops; others are entire towns. Some are so far out in the country you practically have to swing through the trees to get to them; others are in the hub of a city and attract customers from hundreds of miles around. They might be open seasonally, year-round, on weekends, or just as an annual event. But they all have one thing in common: they offer some of the greatest buys around.

These merchandise meccas are located all over the United States and in this book you'll find fabulous places to explore in each one of the contiguous continental states. In a stab at some kind of organization, I've grouped them into nine separate regions, and because it's very hard to get me to be quiet once I've gotten started, I've also included some of the more useful bits of information I've picked up along the way.

These are my secrets about how to shop, how to bid successfully at an auction, how to distinguish the reproduction from the real (a quandary that is growing exponentially each day), what to fix up and what to leave alone, and how to evaluate and then cash in on your collection when you decide it's time to sell.

I've also included a few chapters of sources— places to find, among other things, those hard-to-get parts for a wooden refrigerator or the curved glass to fit into the door of a cabinet, painted glass reproduction *Gone with the Wind* lampshades, even those turkey-claw feet for a piano stool, along with listings of antiques publications—all to help make your hunt for treasures as much fun as the end result.

ANTIQUES
ACROSS AMERICA

CHAPTER ONE

MAKING THE MOST OF A YARD SALE

Yard sales are a worthwhile starting point in this journey because they are at the bottom of the food chain in the ecosystem of antiques. Although dealers complain about them constantly, many routinely spend their weekend mornings chasing around from sale to sale. They may be called garage sales, tag sales, or estate sales in your part of the country, but the basic rules seem to apply everywhere.

You probably already know, if you've been out yard-sale-ing even once, that the early bird really does get the fattest worm, sometimes the only worm. The question then is: how early?

My friend Bobby Jones, who expanded his furniture repair and refinishing business into also selling antiques a few years ago, decided to have a yard sale at his home to pare down some leftovers one weekend. He was sitting in his underwear in his East Hampton kitchen at six in the morning, trying to wake up with a cup of strong black coffee, when two middle-aged women rapped on the kitchen window to get his attention, shouting, as he frantically looked for someplace to hide, "Is this the yard sale?"

I don't think Bobby has ever quite recovered, and I know he's never had another yard sale. But those two women weren't doing themselves any favors, because while they hung around trying to strong-arm him into opening his garage early (the sale was advertised to start at nine), another great yard sale was in full swing a few blocks away.

The point is you want to get going as early as possible, but you don't want to become unpleasantly intrusive. Everybody I know automatically assumes that the rule of etiquette for a yard sale allows you to arrive about an hour in advance of the advertised time. Some dealers try to stretch that particular window of opportunity to two hours, but it usually doesn't pay, I've found. And if an ad says "no early birds," believe it.

If a sale isn't actually up and operating when you arrive, but the boxes are coming out of the house or garage, it's acceptable behavior to walk up and ask if they mind your looking as they work. Most often they won't. Sometimes it even helps to volunteer to tote a bale or two. Once, after helping a charity group set up a yard sale, I was allowed to root through a jewelry box as a thank-you and found a beautiful opal ring.

For dealers, the yard sale game plan is to cover as many sales as possible in the shortest time imaginable—and they'll go to incredible lengths to do it.

One aggressive dealer enlists all the part-timers who work for him every Saturday morning to help with the hunt. Each is armed with a cell phone, and they go off in all directions. When one finds something really good, a call goes out to the dealer who decides instantly if the find is worth buying.

Husband-and-wife dealer duos often operate this way: one stays in the car, motor running, while the other leaps out for a fast look. If nothing is promising, the scout scurries back to the vehicle and they zoom off to the next sale with almost no wasted motion.

Most dealers, I've noticed, no longer lose time loading up large items like furniture. They buy, pay, make sure their purchases are marked "sold," and come back later to pick them up.

Racing around like this really does seem to pay off for some dealers. If the idea of doing it appeals to you, you can cut your lead time by planning your route the night before. Check the obscure streets with a good map and number your stops.

Street-by-street guides with extensive reference listings are worth the investment if you like to yard sale in larger cities. In smaller towns, local newspapers may have giveaway maps, as do most chambers of commerce.

My personal opinion, although I have absolutely nothing to back it up with except my own experience, is that the harder it is to find a yard sale, the lower the probability anything worthwhile will be there when you arrive. It should be the other way around, of course. Our entire Puritan heritage tells us the more effort we put into any one thing, the greater the reward at the end of the line. This may be absolutely true in an ethical or philosophic sense, but it is not so at a yard sale. I have yet to spend an hour following tiny cryptic signs in and out of woods or dead-end streets and come up with anything worthwhile.

However, I've learned it does pay, when you arrive at a yard sale, to stop, park, and leave your car to walk over and check it out more closely, even if it seems initially to be nothing but baby clothes. Most people who are conducting yard sales aren't professionals and they don't think too much about the value of artful display, so the heavy mahogany rocker stays in the garage because it's so awkward to move and the box of grandma's dishes doesn't get unwrapped because it'll take too long to put out the whole set.

I once went to a small yard sale that consisted of nothing more than a few card tables full of nondescript pots and pans, and was about to leave when a neighbor came over to the woman who was running the sale and said, "I'm here to help. Do you have anything you want me to bring out?"

"Just the big box that has all the old lace," she replied.

It was a stellar moment.

Dealers can get a little intense at yard sales and I guess the rest of us should try to be tolerant because they're not just shopping for fun; they're out to earn a living. Still, that doesn't give anyone the right to run over you and unfortunately, some highly competitive dealers will try. If you find something desirable that you want to buy, do not let it leave your hand for a moment until you've found the person running the sale and actually paid for it. If you're going to buy a piece of furniture that's too big to carry over to the seller, this is the time for the roll of masking tape and a black marker you naturally bring with you every time you go to a yard sale. Slap a piece of masking tape on your found object and mark it "Sold" along with your name. Then there's no room for unpleasant misunderstandings to occur.

I don't like to leave furniture or anything else at a sale after I've paid for it unless I absolutely have to. If it's a bargain, all too often a dealer will come by and offer the seller more than you've already paid. Human nature being what it is, sometimes that's just too tempting to resist, so if you know you've gotten a super buy, take it with you right away.

For a while I was being followed around at yard sales by a dealer whose technique was to shout "I already bought that!" every time she saw me pick up something interesting. The first few times it happened, I believed her, but then I realized she was doing the same thing regularly and to a lot of other people as well.

The next time she tried this, I shouted back, "Have you already paid for it?" When she grudgingly admitted she had not, I refused to give the merchandise up, and from then on, that particular game was over. Several people have told me the same thing has happened to them in other parts of the country.

But what also seems to be a growing trend on the plus side is the neighborhood sale, or town sale, in which everyone in a given area participates in a one-day yard sale, often paying a small fee or turning over a percentage of the proceeds to charity. These are the kinds of yard sales to hunt for, because if a couple of hundred, or couple of thousand yard sales are going on all at once in a town or city, your chances of discovering a major find increases dramatically. These town-wide yard sales seem to be increasingly popular in the northeast; this past summer, I found them in dozens of small suburban communities in New Jersey, Pennsylvania, Long Island, upper New York State, and Connecticut. For example, Sea Cliff, New Jersey, does this as a benefit for the local volunteer ambulance corps, while Bloomsbury, New Jersey, raises funds for the P.T.A.

I've heard about sales in Vermont, New Hampshire, Massachusetts, and I picked up an article that said White Cloud, Kansas, has such a great annual town-wide yard sale on Labor Day weekend that it's worth the drive from almost anywhere.

The ultimate, all-time, award-winning, mother of all yard sales is, of course, the 450-mile sale that occurs every August and follows a course through Kentucky, Tennessee, Alabama and a little bit of Georgia. (See Page 109 for details.)

In Norwich, Vermont, they go everyone one better and have a free yard sale. On a summer weekend, the entire community brings its discards to the town square to give away to anyone who wants them. It's a major event and the party atmosphere, I'm told, is enhanced by free refreshments. Friends of mine who've gone to this sale say they've found absolutely wonderful antiques, things the previous owners didn't consider valuable and probably would have discarded at the dump. If you're interested, check with the Earth Right Institute in Norwich for dates. They don't always do it annually; sometimes they skip a year.

You could do worse than check out your local dump once in a while. Dump scavenging, or bin diving as it's known in England, is becoming more and more acceptable. People who used to furtively lug treasures back from their local dump now do it openly and brag abut it. Some of the best dumps in the country have achieved a kind of celebrity status, especially since the practice of recycling has evolved into a necessary civic virtue.

Good Things to Look For at Yard Sales

1. Van Briggle pottery. This Colorado Springs, Colorado pottery, in business about one hundred years, first developed and specializes in a distinctive turquoise blue glaze. Like other American art pottery, even fairly recent pieces are hot collectibles, and the older pieces can bring more than a thousand dollars. It's all marked Van Briggle on the bottom.

2. Embroidered pillowcases. Actually, almost any kind of hand done needlework is extremely collectible, but those old pillowcases, the ones grandma used to embroider with colored embroidery floss, are now selling for $15 to $45 per pair, depending upon the quality of the work and design.

3. Silverplate anything. Although prices for old silverplate are no longer soaring as high as they did a couple of years ago, this much-disdained second cousin to sterling—you can tell because it's all marked plate or I.S. or E.N.P.S.—is now valuable. Check any of the several silverplate price guides. You should be looking for serving pieces as well as cutlery. If it's blackened, it's usually cheap, and it's not hard to clean (see chapter 11 on repairs).

4. Doorknobs. The best, of course, are the glass doorknobs in purple, green, or clear faceted designs. They sell for up to $100 in working condition. Old-fashioned white ceramic knobs sell for at least $15 a set; a real prize is the Bennington doorknob, a swirl of brown shades in glass that mimics Bennington pottery. At least $50 a set. Old door locks and escutcheon plates are good, too, as is anything like hinges, knobs, or any other hardware in wrought iron or brass.

5. White ironstone china, any kind, any shape. The only thing to watch out for are the dings and cracks that this serviceable and sturdy china acquires because it was so well used. Look for all the pieces that were part of the bathing set. You've probably seen the pitchers and bowls that used to sit on washstands; but these sets often came with up to a dozen pieces—accessories included a smaller pitcher, a glass or mug, a covered jug for used water, a lidded potty, soap dish, and small jars or trays. Kitchen items—plates, platters, mugs—are also great finds.

6. Pewter. A lot of pewter gets tossed into the junk boxes at yard sales because it looks like worn-out silverplate. It's all collectible and if you pick up an Early American piece, you've really found a major prize. Expect a few dings and other signs of wear in old pieces, because pewter is very soft. It cleans up nicely with toothpaste.

7. Architectural bits and pieces. A piece of elaborate wooden molding, a single shutter, perhaps one side of a cupola, or even a newel post—old architectural fragments are becoming hot collectibles and have achieved the status of folk art. Just make sure it's old.

8. Jewel Tea china. This inexpensive dinnerware was particularly popular in the Midwest, although it appears all over the country. It was sold or given as a premium by the Jewel Tea Company, a home delivery firm that sold everything from vanilla extract to candied fruit. The autumn leaf pattern is the most common, but there are several other designs. There are price guides.

9. Old photographs. Any kind of old photograph, whether it includes a family pose or just a landscape, is a sought-after collectible. Some can get extremely high prices as works of art, but even garden variety old photographs sell well, and dealers like to stock them.

10. Beacon blankets. These blankets, usually Indian-style designs in bold patterns and bright colors, were manufactured in the thirties and forties, and although they are not as prized as the Hudson's Bay blankets, they are still very collectible.

The East Hampton, Long Island dump is practically legendary. For a while, its recyclable area was even covered with a huge yellow-and-white striped tent, the kind commonly seen at society weddings. This dump has been the subject of stories in the *New York Times* and I know, personally, that antiques worth thousands of dollars have turned up there.

The Aspen, Colorado, dump has the same type of luster, and employs dump workers who are as knowledgeable as many antiques dealers. Back east again in Wellesley, Massachusetts, the dump now runs its own antique flea market with salvaged treasures priced for sale.

If you're up for bin diving, concentrate on dumps that adjoin exclusive, expensive living areas. If possible, make friends with the gatekeepers and find out what they do with the really good stuff. Often, they may already have arrangements in place with local dealers, but you might be able to get in on the game.

CHAPTER TWO

Northern Coastal Region

Connecticut, Massachusetts, Rhode Island, Maine, Vermont, New Hampshire

This part of the country has some of the best antique resources in the United States. There are probably more shops in this area than anywhere else, and on summer weekends it often appears as though every other open field is hosting a flea market or antique show. There are still bargains to be found in these states but even the pricier shops are worth visiting as a learning experience.

CONNECTICUT

Woodbury Outdoor Market

There are some states where fine antiques are the norm rather than the exception. Connecticut, particularly the Route 7 corridor that runs from south to north along the eastern side of the state, is chock full of exquisite antiques shops. They are filled with beautiful pieces in pristine condition that are, predictably, expensive. Windsor chairs are so hot right now that the price for an average example has jumped from $500-$600 to $1,200-$1,500 in the past few years, and Connecticut seems to have many good ones.

What makes all this interesting to those of us who can't or don't want to pay retail for a Windsor chair, is that your chances of buying a good antique here are higher than you might expect. Anything that isn't absolutely primo gets passed over by the top-drawer dealers. And that means that in some of the smaller shops and outdoor markets, you will do very well.

The Woodbury Outdoor Market, located at the intersection of Route 6 and 64 just outside the town itself, is one of the best spots in the state to hunt for antiques.

It is clearly not one of the professional flea markets, although there are the usual dealers in discount towels, soap, and wind-up toys. But the antiques dealers don't come here equipped with fancy vans and tents from which to sell. Instead, you're more liable to see beach umbrellas or homemade tarp squares rigged as sunshades.

That's probably a good indication of bargain potential, and the bargains certainly were there when I checked it out. This seemed an excellent place for furniture because the prices were so low, and the dealers told me they thought it was a slow weekend with fewer people selling than usual.

Dealers change every weekend, although there are, of course, some regulars who have been in business here for twenty-seven years.

The market opens officially at 7:00 A.M. on Saturdays, but dealers and customers will be doing business by 5:30 A.M. It closes up at around 2 P.M. so it's a morning experience.

You can enjoy that experience every Saturday for most of the year, although the season winds down in November and doesn't really get into full swing again until April. There are occasional Saturdays during the winter months when the market is open if the weather's good.

TO GET THERE: Take Interstate 84 and get off at Exit 15; the market is nearby at the junction of Routes 6 and 64.

FOR MORE INFORMATION: Telephone Diane and Don Heavens at 1-203-263-2841.

Treasure Factory

This is one of those mythic places, a huge old building loaded to the gills with "stuff." This building was once the most important symbol of progress for miles around; it was the manufacturing site for the

Amston automobile, one of the early horseless carriages.

Today, the old factory just off Route 66 in the western part of the state doesn't seem to have changed too much, except for the fact that it now holds four floors filled with antiques organized in no particular order at all.

Some of the prices on the more obvious antiques were average retail or even higher. However, there were lots of goodies that were undervalued and it was clear that bargaining was acceptable.

Everything is such a jumble that you'll have to plan to spend a couple of hours just digging through, but there are rewards like the painted Hitchcock chair in perfect condition for $35. A very nice nineteenth-century accountant's desk also interested me. It was pretty rough, but at $50, worth the price to fix up.

Don't wear light-colored clothes; it's pretty grungy. It's open Saturdays and Sundays 11 to 5 year-round.

TO GET THERE: Hebron is east of Hartford off Interstate 2 to Route 66, then south on Route 85.

FOR MORE INFORMATION: Telephone 1-860-228-0111 or 1-860-642-7867.

ADDENDUM: While you're in the area, check out the small town of East Hampton, on Route 66 just west of Hebron. This looks to me as though it's going to become one of those all-antiques towns. There are at least eight shops that have opened in the past few years, including a multi-dealer mall that is located in an old bank. Prices are quite reasonable.

Elephant's Trunk Flea Market

This is the larger of Connecticut's two top outdoor markets, and while the Woodbury market is open on Saturdays only, this one is open just on Sundays. Some dealers like to set up shop at both. Generally, the market opens for the season in April and will stay open through the winter months as long as the weather permits.

Like many other flea markets there are some vendors selling new merchandise, but the real attraction is always the antiques dealers, all of whom say they do very well because of the high turnout.

TO GET THERE: From Interstate 84 take Exit 7 to Route 7, then 6 miles, turn right, also Route 7. You'll see the flea market on the left 3.8 miles down the road.

FOR MORE INFORMATION: Telephone 1-860-355-1448.

MASSACHUSETTS

Brimfield Antiques Market

This is the mother of all markets and if you're even mildly interested in antiques, it's the one place you should go at least once in your life. Dealers and avid collectors flock to Brimfield three times a year— in May, July, and September. During each market three to four thousand dealers will crowd into the fields around this small town, attracting more than a million people every year.

It is, according to Brimfield writer-in-residence Bob Brown, who publishes a newspaper and has written several books about Brimfield, "a giant warehouse for small shops all over the country. They come here every year to buy the goods that will carry them through the year."

Brown says the May show is usually the largest, and the best to see if you can come to only one. Because it's the start of a new season, dealers are anxious to sell and bring a lot of wares.

However, May can be cold and rainy. Brown says you can count on rain for at least one of the six selling days and suggests visitors remember to bring warm clothing, raincoats, and umbrellas as well as comfortable walking shoes.

Currently there are twenty-two participating fields, or separate markets. Each has individual admission policies: some are free; some charge. The first fields open on Tuesday, with more following each day until Friday, when all are open. Fridays and Saturdays are always the biggest selling days, but the dealers who are the most serious buyers will be out there late Monday night with flashlights, and every night thereafter just before a field opens.

J & J, the largest and oldest of the markets, is right in the center of town. It's operated by sisters Jill Reid Lukash and Judith Reid Mathieu and is the linchpin of the Brimfield shows. Their father, Gordon Reid, actually started the market in 1959 after he had visited an outdoor antiques show created by a man who'd been inspired by the Paris Flea Market.

(You probably already know that "flea market" is a translation of the French term *marches aux puces,* so named because vintage clothes were part of the Paris market and all too often were hosts to fleas.)

Dealers often wear both hats at Brimfield, buying one day and then selling the next. By the time the big weekend crowds arrive, some merchandise may have changed hands two or three times. It's imperative to know your prices before you go; if you can, shop a few days before the weekend.

It's mandatory to follow this advice from every Brimfield veteran: you absolutely must make room reservations well in advance—six months to a year ahead is not unreasonable. Sleeping space of any kind, even campground spots, are impossible to get when it's close to show time, so unless you want to drive a hundred miles to a motel, plan well ahead.

TO GET THERE: Take Interstate 84 to Mass. Route 20 and follow the steady stream of traffic toward Sturbridge. The route is well marked.

FOR MORE INFORMATION: Telephone J & J Promotions, 1-413-245-3436, or write for Bob Brown's book,

The Collector's Paradise, Brimfield Publications, P.O. Box 442, Brimfield, MA 01010 ($17.95).

Southampton Antiques

Southampton is a town so small it's not even on my map. However, it's close to Northampton, home of Smith College, and relatively easy to find.

The hunt is going to be worth it. Owner Bruce Cummings has stocked five floors full of very specialized antiques—good Victorian and turn-of-the-century oak furniture. He has very few small items, although there is the odd decorative accessory.

This shop has been in business since 1971 and at this location since 1981; dealers love it because the two smaller barns on the property are stocked with furniture in "as is" condition. Cummings says he doesn't sell "basket case" furniture pieces too badly in need of repair, but those that need just a little work are priced reasonably.

Cummings also will do a customized videotape for customers who are looking for specialized merchandise. He says his videos generally run thirty-five minutes and will focus on pieces that are currently available in his shop. You tell him what you want and he'll document what he has available. The cost for the video is $25.

The store is open Thursdays, Fridays, and Saturdays, 10 to 5, and is closed for the entire month of August.

TO GET THERE: Southampton Antiques, 171 College Highway, Southampton, Mass., 01073 (Exit 3 off Massachusetts Turnpike)

FOR MORE INFORMATION: Telephone 1-413-527-1022

Wellfleet Flea Market

This flea market gets high marks from both buyers and sellers. It is considered the best flea market in the Cape Cod area and has approximately 200 dealers selling here on Saturdays and Sundays as well as holiday Mondays. Open from mid-April through October. Admission $1 or $2 per carload depending upon the date. Lots of antiques! Good seafood too.

TO GET THERE: Wellfleet is located between Hyannis and Provincetown, on the narrow spit that curves out into the Atlantic Ocean. Take Route 6 east and look for the Drive-In Theater sign.

FOR MORE INFORMATION: Wellfleet Drive-In, P.O. Box 811, Wellfleet, MA 02667, or telephone 1-508-349-2520.

RHODE ISLAND

Buck's Unlimited

Every once in a while you will find a dealer who specializes in one unique antiques category. Usually, people who focus their attention this way know everything there is to know about their chosen subject and they're almost always fascinating to talk with. Ron "Buck" Rogers deals primarily in fire department memorabilia, including uniforms, equipment, even those old-fashioned square red alarm boxes that used to stand on every corner. He's a full-time fireman himself, and operates his shop on the weekends as an avocation. Occasionally he does shows.

When I caught up with him, he had for sale a white leather chief's helmet from Boston, which I would have bought myself, except for the fact that I would have had no place left to put it except on my head.

Because he moves around a lot and his schedule changes, you should call first to make sure he's going to be in before you travel to his East Greenwich, Rhode Island, shop. Fire memorabilia collectors will find him, and his shop, to be a national treasure.

TO GET THERE: Buck's Unlimited, 71 Herbert St., East Greenwich, RI, 02818
FOR MORE INFORMATION: Telephone 1-401-884-9058
ADDENDUM: Ask Buck to point you in the direction of the other antiques shops in East Greenwich. They're small, but interesting.

General Stanton Flea Market

This is a flea market that dealers like to keep secret if possible because a search of the merchandise here can yield some really amazing rewards. Janet Falcone, who has owned and operated it for thirty-one years, says that she knows of one buyer who found a painting that later sold at Sotheby's for $450,000, and another who bought an etching that fetched $55,000.

Not everyone is going to strike it rich, but the assortment of dealers who bring their wares here is varied indeed. Some come from as far away as New York City and there are plenty of dealers who use this flea market as their primary source.

Like most flea markets, Falcone's does have the usual Fuller brush kinds of things; however, this is a family-rated market. There are no racy videotapes or funny posters. The surroundings are pleasant, filled with shade trees and ocean breezes.

Although it's open from 8 to 4 on Saturdays and Sundays, most dealers don't show up until Sunday. Compared to the rest of the eastern flea markets, this one has a short season. It opens in early May and most of the antiques dealers end their season by mid-September.

Note: For the past twenty-five years, Falcone has owned the adjacent General Stanton Inn, the oldest continuously operating inn in the United States and the home of Revolutionary War hero and statesman Joseph Stanton. Rooms are $85 to $95 per night. Admission to the flea market is free although there is a $1.00 parking fee.

TO GET THERE: General Stanton Flea Market, P.O. Box 222, Charlestown, RI, 02813. Charlestown is just south of Route 1, which runs along the coastline and eventually connects with Interstate 95.
FOR MORE INFORMATION: Telephone 1-401-364-8888

Blue Flag Antiques

Sarah Harkness and her partner, John Nelson, own this small shop in one of the most beautiful corners of the United States. Little Compton, Rhode Island is about as far east as you can get in the state, on a tiny yet sublime spit of land. There doesn't seem to be a house around that doesn't have *Architectural Digest* potential and the antiques are classically elegant. Sarah's shop is small, but she has some very nice and unusual things, fairly priced. Other than her shop, and a group of a half-dozen or so in Tiverton's Four Corners area, right down the road, there are not a lot of antiques shops here. I still say check it out; it's just too pretty to pass up.

And, twice a year, Sarah and some other local dealers gather at the Little Compton Antiques Show sponsored by the Village Improvement Society. These shows are worth the trip by themselves. The Tiverton Four Corners dealers also host a summer antiques show.

TO GET THERE: From Fall River, Massachusetts, take Route 138 south along the shoreline; it changes to

Rhode Island Route 77, follow 77 to Tiverton or Little Compton.

FOR MORE INFORMATION: Write to 601 West Main Road, Little Compton, RI, 02837, or telephone 1-401-635-8707.

MAINE

Bridgton and Environs

Because Maine has the smallest population of the New England states, antiques shops in the upper regions of the state are sparse. Dealers find their wares through auctions and flea markets. The town of Bridgton consequently is unique because it is composed of so many antique shops. For ten years the centerpiece of the Main Street shops in Bridgton has been Wales & Hamblen, a co-op with thirty-eight dealers, most of whom specialize in small antiques. One of the mall's features is an extensive collection of antique books. Because the large building is unheated, the mall is only open from Memorial Day through leaf season in October, six days a week, closed Mondays.

Ricker House in Bridgton features seventeenth- and eighteenth-century antique furniture; Hidden Brook Antiques has small items. In North Bridgton there's the Paper Chase and the Lampshade Shop featuring antique lighting fixtures. In nearby Naples, just a few miles away on Route 302, there are several stores including the Sudbury Schoolmarm, the Naples Gallery, and the Jones Gallery, a shop and museum of glass and ceramics. In Harrison, look for Hermitage Antiques featuring Victorian and early American furniture and Mr. Oak, a shop that features refinished oak furniture.

Most of the area shops do close for the year after the leaf season ends in October and reopen again in the spring.

TO GET THERE: These small towns are almost due north of Portland along Route 302 and Maine 117. Pick up 302 off Interstate 95.

FOR MORE INFORMATION: Telephone The Ricker House, 1-207-647-5069; Wales & Hamblen, 1-207-647-3840.

Wells Antique Mart

Route One, which parallels Interstate 95 along the New England coastline, has become a popular site for antiques shops, including Maine's best antiques malls. Wells, with eighty dealers, features mainly small items and is open year-round, seven days a week, 9 to 5. Well-established with a loyal following, the mall has been operating from this location for eighteen years.

TO GET THERE: North on Interstate 95 to Wells on Route One.

FOR MORE INFORMATION: Telephone Wells Antique Mart, 1-207-646-8153

Arundel Antiques

Just a little farther south on Route One, near Kennebunkport, this two-story mall has two hundred booths and is open year-round, seven days a week. In the winter, it's open from 9 to 5; in summer, 8 to 6. Try to get there for the annual St. Patrick's Day sale, in which all the dealers participate.

TO GET THERE: Follow Route One south to Kennebunk and Kennebunkport.

FOR MORE INFORMATION: Telephone 1-207-985-7965.

Montsweag Flea Market

Located in Woolwich, Maine on Route One, this outdoor flea market is a prime source for many of the antiques dealers along the coastline roadway. Open on weekends beginning with Mother's Day weekend if the weather's good, and closing at the end of October after leaf season, this market celebrated its twentieth anniversary in 1996. On Saturdays and Sundays, seventy-five percent of the dealers here sell collectibles and antiques. During June, July, and August, the market is also open on

Wednesdays and Fridays. On Wednesday, antiques and collectibles only are sold.

TO GET THERE: Woolwich is only about fifteen miles from Freeport, Maine, which is worth noting because Freeport has the best outlet shops in the northeast, including a rare Brooks Brothers and a Ralph Lauren outlet. L.L. Bean, the famous Maine sporting goods store, is the cornerstone of Freeport; the outlet shops and the Route One antiques dealers have been benefiting from the growing enthusiasm for this area. Take Route One, north from Freeport.

FOR MORE INFORMATION: Norma Scopino, owner, Montsweag Flea Market. Telephone 1-207-443-2809.

VERMONT

Norm's Antiques and Collectibles and Old Barn Museum

When dealers say "I bought it from this old guy" as an explanation, what they usually mean is that they're not prepared to divulge their source on pain of death. However, there is indeed a Norm and his shop in the small town of Taftsville, near Woodstock, Vermont, is fantastic.

He's one of the few dealers who's managed to scout out some good Early American furniture. He also has an amazingly extensive collection of old sleighs and horse buggies, most of them extremely reasonably priced. I know a lot of other parts of the country in which Norm could double his money on them. The buggies and sleighs are outdoors; inside, there are three floors of really nice merchandise. He's only open from May 15 through December, and you might want to call before you make travel plans to be sure he's going to be available.

TO GET THERE: Norman Boynton, Route 4, Box 51, Taftsville, VT, 05073. Take Route 4 West toward Woodstock from Interstate 91, which runs north and south. Taftsville is directly on Route 4 about three miles east of Woodstock.

FOR MORE INFORMATION: Telephone 1-802-457-3009 or 1-802-295-3004.

Quechee Gorge Village Antique Center

Quechee Gorge is Vermont's answer to the Grand Canyon, and a tourist attraction that draws visitors from every part of the country. In the nearby town, this large and sprawling antique mall and country store is a major attraction, too. It has loads of activities to interest children, so families can make a day of it. When you enter the complex, gifts and crafts are off to the left; when you turn right you find 450 dealer booths, most featuring what dealers like to refer to as "smalls"—glassware, lamps, curios, and the like. Because of the rapid turnover, especially during the summer, dealers do well here and the result is that prices are generally quite good. Open year-round, seven days a week, 10 to 5.

TO GET THERE: P.O. Box 0730, Quechee, VT 05059. West on Route 4 off Exit 1 from Interstate 89, between White River Junction and Woodstock, Vermont.
FOR MORE INFORMATION: Telephone 1-800-438-5565.

The Antiques Collaborative

This is one of the most attractive group shops you'll ever see. The merchandise is elegant and up-scale and the room settings have a designer look. There are ninety dealers in thirty showrooms—a total of 12,000 square feet—filled with fine European and American furniture. The prices aren't cheap, but they're not as expensive as they would be in other shops of this caliber. The collection of estate jewelry and oriental carpets is outstanding.

Open seven days a week year-round, 10 to 5. There is an on-site restaurant with dining gallery.

TO GET THERE: Located on Route 4, at P.O. Box 565, Quechee, VT, 05059. Close to the junction of Interstates 89 and 91, six miles east of Woodstock, VT.
FOR MORE INFORMATION: Telephone 1-802-296-5858.

NEW HAMPSHIRE

This is one of the most active antique-trading states in the country. There are dozens and dozens of small independent shops throughout the state as well as an extremely busy dealers' association.

The first week of August is always Antique Week in New Hampshire. It started when the New Hampshire Antique Dealers' Association began to sponsor an antiques show in Manchester that is still regarded as the keystone event of the week. Now, other shows are conducted during the same week in Manchester, along with a number of major auctions.

Show merchandise is top quality and consequently, expensive—a great place to see what the best really looks like even if you can't afford to spend thousands for a blanket chest or a single chair. But the real benefit for canny antiquers are the dozens of special sales in malls and small shops, plus a lot of yard sales and flea markets, all piggybacking nearby during the same week, hoping to attract some of the thousands of people traveling into the state for all the auctions and shows.

At other times of the year, check into the group of shops that line New Hampshire's Route 4, from Concord to Portsmouth. Known as Antique Alley, there are dozens of shops along this 20-mile stretch of road.

Colonial Plaza Antique Markets

This is a dual market—an antique mall that is open seven days a week, plus an outdoor Sunday market. The antique mall itself has sixty-five dealers and is open year-round with the exception of Christmas Day and New Year's Day. The outdoor market opens in April and closes after leaf season ends in New Hampshire, generally around the end of October. An average of 50 dealers usually show up for the Sunday market, which opens at first light.

TO GET THERE: This market is located in the middle of West Lebanon's mall area on Route 12A, just off the junction of Routes 89 and 91.

FOR MORE INFORMATION: Write to Colonial Plaza Antiques, 23 Airport Road, West Lebanon, New Hampshire, 03784; or telephone 1-603-298-7712

Prospect Hill Antiques

This huge barn, located in the small town of Georges Mills, is filled with three floors of extremely interesting antiques, including some fine furniture from Ireland, England, and other parts of Europe as well as American pieces. Owned and operated by Ronald Sullivan for fifteen years, the barn is definitely worth a visit, especially in October because the annual sale offers discounts of ten to forty percent on everything in the store.

TO GET THERE: Exit 12A from Route 89 to Georges Mills, which is about a half-hour drive from Lebanon.

FOR MORE INFORMATION: Write P.O. Box 359, Georges Mills, New Hampshire 03751; or telephone 1-603-763-9676

Burlwood Antique Center

The most interesting feature of this large tri-level 170-dealer mall is a huge furniture-only area on the bottom floor where there are always at least a few great buys. The mall has two other floors of smaller antiques as well, including some very nice estate jewelry. Open only six months of the year, from May 1 through October 31.

TO GET THERE: Take Interstate 93 to Exit 23, then Route 104 East eight miles to junction of 104 and Route 3.

FOR MORE INFORMATION: Telephone 1-603-279-6387.

Lake Winnipesaukee Antique District

The Burlwood Antique Center is just one of the more than fifty separate antiques shops that are located in the area north and east of Lake Winnepesaukee. Many of them are located along Routes 25, 16, and 109 or 109A. Any one of the area's shops will be able to give you a map and directions to all the rest.

CHAPTER THREE

BIDDING—AND WINNING— AT AUCTIONS

Apart from yard sales, the only other arena in which you're liable to run up against a dealer "mano a mano" is the auction. And if you've ever had a dealer get the better of you at a yard sale, competing against one in an auction can be very satisfying because now it's payback time.

We're not going to talk about the elite auctions at places like Sotheby's or Christie's where furniture and jewelry routinely draw bids in the thousands or hundreds of thousands of dollars. The Jacqueline Kennedy Onassis auction was the penultimate example, and most of us probably will never attend one of these way-too-posh affairs.

I had planned on attending the Rudolf Nureyev auction in New York that was held about two years before the Onassis one, because the advertised prices actually seemed reachable. Nureyev's ballet slippers—he never threw any of them away, it seems, and had hundreds stashed in his closets— were estimated to bring $40 to $60 per pair, and I had great dreams of buying one pair and displaying them under a glass bell with a few ballet programs. Well, something came up and I never did make the auction, which was just as well because those slippers with the $60 estimate went for thousands—six to eight thousand to be exact—per pair, yes, each pair. Had I been there I probably would have had a coronary.

However, many auctions are very different from these and draw everyday people like you and me. The auctions most of us are likely to attend are estate or farm sales, or community fund-raisers, where the majority of the spectators aren't in the trade and you don't need to take out a second mortgage in order to be able to participate. Most of these auctions won't make you purchase a catalog because they don't have them. At best, you'll get a printed list of the items to be sold along with their lot numbers.

These auctions can be fun. Sometimes they become the most popular form of community entertainment, with an audience held in thrall as people bid on everything from snowplow blades to forties footwear. They're very informal, and you don't have to worry that if you scratch your nose, you'll have bought something. These "anything-and-everything" auctions can become a little wearisome, though, as you sit through endless boxes of old knitting yarn and hair curlers, waiting for a few antiques to come up for sale, but prices tend to be extremely low and worth the wait because most dealers don't want to bother investing all that time for just a few items. Dealers prefer the specialized auctions, generally conducted by professional auctioneers who operate in one local area and may do as many as two or three antiques or estate auctions every week.

At this kind of auction, the average person almost always has an edge over any dealer. That advantage is created by the dealer's need to resell.

Let's say both you and your friendly local neighborhood antique shop owner are interested in a cobalt blue glass vase that's coming up for sale. You've both looked it over and you both think it's worth about $100. The dealer can't really pay much more than $50 and still make a reasonable profit, so you can top that bid by a few dollars and acquire your vase at a price that's dramatically lower than what you'd expect to pay in a shop.

At any auction, there's really only one major rule—never ever bid on anything you haven't checked out thoroughly in advance. If you ignore this rule, you are almost certainly headed for disaster. Everybody, no matter what their level of expertise, tries to challenge this rule sooner or later, and just as inevitably loses. It is one of the few absolutes in an otherwise fairly unstructured world. This is why at auctions you may see dealers practically crawling up to the podium on their hands and knees while the auction is in progress; they're trying to get a good look at something they missed earlier.

The last time I bid without inspecting in advance, I bought a fabulous Persian carpet for $150. I'd arrived at the auction late and walked in the door just as the bidding for the carpet began. I was elated when I won because I knew I could resell it for at least a thousand more than I'd paid for it. Congratulating myself on my keen eye, I sauntered over to pay for it after the auction ended and looked at it closely for the first time. My knees literally went weak and my life all but started to flash before my eyes. It was a good carpet, even a great carpet, and it was unquestionably authentic and old. The only problem was, it was in pieces. The entire back of the carpet was a maze of masking tape. I don't think there was an intact section more than a couple of feet square.

Let that be a lesson. Always, always, always get to the auction in plenty of time to inspect everything you might want to bid on. If it's a chair, or another piece of furniture, turn it upside down if you can, look underneath and behind it, pull out the drawers, and try to check every square inch for breaks, patches, or replacements.

Dealers always carry small, strong flashlights and you should, too. Auction rooms are often a little dim, and even in bright light, a flashlight will illuminate a problem you might have overlooked. A pen and a

notebook are equally important pre-auction inspection tools. You'll want to write down a quick description of each item you want to bid on, and along with
it, the lot number of the piece and the maximum
amount you're prepared to pay.

(While we're on the subject of supplies, this is a
good time to mention that you'll want to bring along
your trusty roll of masking tape and your marking
pen, as well as some flattened cardboard boxes and
old newspapers to pack fragile things. At auction
houses, packing materials are either in short supply
or nonexistent.)

Auctioneers sell at the rate of forty to one hundred
lots per hour. That means that even at the most lei-
surely auction, you're not going to have more than
a minute and a half, at most, to bid and win. A lot
of auctions move quickly and you might not have
even a minute to bid and rebid. Writing down in
advance the top price you're willing to pay acts as an
automatic brake on auction fever; it's awfully easy to
get carried away in the excitement of those few intense seconds and just keep bidding.

Because auctions are so fast and furious, you have
to pay close attention to what the auctioneer says.
Is he selling that set of four chairs for one price, or
is the bidding per chair, which actually means four
times that price when the dust settles?

Some auction houses now add what they call a
"buyer's premium" to each sale. It can be ten percent, or even fifteen, and while that doesn't sound

like a lot, it is an important factor to keep in mind when you're bidding because it makes the price substantially higher at the end of the game. Let's say you bid $200 for a small cupboard. With a buyer's premium of fifteen percent, you're actually bidding $230, an important distinction, especially if you're spending a lot of money at one time.

If you make a mistake in the course of the auction and discover, a little too late, that you waved your paddle at Lot 145, the box of rolling pins, when you were really after Lot 146, the salt-glazed crock, let the auctioneer know immediately. Generally, if you fess up right away in front of everyone, the worst that will happen is you'll feel embarrassed but the item will be sold again. If you wait until the auction's over to protest, they're not going to let you off the hook.

Any auctioneer will tell you that even though twenty people may offer bids at the start, competition will narrow quickly to two, or at most three, bidders. Forget about all that old movie and TV stuff about making your bid as unobtrusive as possible. It doesn't happen in real life. Signal with your paddle or bidding number; wave your hand and shout if you have to.

You can negotiate a little with the auctioneer, using hand signals to convey your bid. If the auctioneer is asking for a $100 bid, and you aren't willing to go that high but will offer $50, you can tell that to the auctioneer by moving your hand back and forth horizontally—"cutting" the bid in half.

You can also indicate your bid by raising your fingers. If the auctioneer is asking for $300, you can indicate your bid by raising one finger for $100 or two for $200 and so on.

When you're in the middle of a bidding contest with one or two competitors, the worst thing you can do is to weigh each bid. If you're after an oak washstand and you've decided $150 is as high as you're prepared to go, make your bids as quickly as possible; don't take the time to deliberate. If you bid slowly, your competition will think you're dithering and hope to force you out by increasing the next bid you'll have to make. Bid as quickly as you can and screech to a halt when you hit your pre-set spending limit. You may decide to try one or two last bids that are above your limit and that's fine. But what you want to avoid is the "I must have this at all costs" frenzy, because that can lead to a bidding spurt that ends with your washstand costing you about twice as much as it would in an expensive antique shop.

Less reputable auctions sometimes attempt to encourage bidding to get out of control by planting shills in the audience. Or, the shills may be operating independently of the auctioneers. Often, they are consigners who own some of the merchandise that's being sold that night and are inflating the bids to get the most they can for their goods. In really crooked auctions, the shills work directly with the auctioneer and there may be as many as six scattered throughout the audience.

Rigging bids at an auction is illegal, of course, and if caught these people would go straight to jail, but artificially inflating bids is difficult to prove, especially in the middle of an auction.

You can protect yourself from shills with a fairly simple technique. If you suspect someone is hyping your bids, quickly bid on a lot you don't mind losing and bid for it as rapidly as you can. The shill or shills will think they've got the proverbial live one and happily match and up your bids just as fast as you do. You want to create the impression while you're doing this that you're so enthusiastic you're going to be doing this forever, so don't hesitate. Then, just as abruptly as you can, drop out. The shill will, in all likelihood, top your bid and be left with that last artificial bid hanging out there in midair. Since the last thing any shill wants is to actually win in a bidding contest, after you do this two or three times, the shills will get the message and leave you alone.

Pulling this kind of stunt can be immensely enjoyable especially if the auctioneer is in on the scam. If you've caught out a shill who is working with the house, you'll find the auctioneer practically pleading with you to make another bid. This can be a little dangerous. You don't want to end up buying something just to prove a point.

Don't rush into this kind of gambit at an auction until you feel that you're familiar with the tempo of the room and have identified all the main players. And don't bid on a lot unless it's an item you've planned to try to win anyway.

You can't get hurt too badly if you keep to your preset spending limit and have checked out the merchandise thoroughly in advance. No one will be able to lure you into foolish overbidding, no matter how cleverly the house has tried to stack the deck.

If you watch dealers at an auction, you'll notice that even though they may nod to friends or wave and smile, they're not engaging in a lot of small talk. In fact, they may seem positively antisocial and focused totally on the auctioneer. Concentration is important. When you chat with the person next to you, it's awfully easy to lose track of where you are in the sale process, and first thing you know, something you really wanted to bid on is going to sail right past before you can think to get your mouth open or your hand up.

I didn't really understand this for years, and it seemed I was always playing catch-up at auctions. Then one evening I greeted another dealer who was kind enough to let me know that the reason he wasn't going to come over and sit next to me was that chatting would interfere with buying. I tried following his lead that night and found he was right. I did a lot better at bidding when I kept my mouth shut.

When the bidding is over and you've won, unless the item you've purchased is so small that it can be handed over to you immediately, try to get to the post-auction pick-up area immediately with your roll of masking tape and mark it. The lot you just bought should already be marked with the lot number and your bidding number. You'll want to add your name and the word *sold*. Especially at farm auctions or smaller estate sales, it's all too easy for major confusion to develop when everyone rushes over to collect their goods at the end. Once I became the unwilling and unwitting owner of a large, sad-eyed, stuffed antelope head because it had been given the wrong bidder's number.

When you've purchased something valuable and breakable that needs extra protection on the way home, here's a great technique I learned. Take a full-size newspaper—not the tabloid size but the kind with large double pages—and crumble two sheets together into a sort of log about the same length as the cardboard box you're going to use as your container. Take a third sheet of the same size paper and place the two crumpled sheets diagonally across it. Beginning at the corner in front of you, roll and wrap the crumpled "log" inside the third sheet to make a firm but flexible log about three or four inches in diameter. Wedge this log in the bottom of the box, and continue to make others, fitting them in until the bottom of the box is filled. Take the piece you need to protect and wrap it in a double sheet of paper the same size. Now, take another sheet and wrap it all over again. Place the wrapped piece on the log layer, anchoring it in place with more crumpled newspaper. Surround it with crumpled paper until the layer is completely filled. Make more logs and add another layer of them on top. You can continue layering rolled logs and double-wrapped merchandise until the box is filled. This takes a lot of newspaper and you won't be able to pack a lot of things into one box, but it is a sure-fire technique.

How do you find auctions? There are probably dozens of them within easy driving distance of your home every week. Look for the giveaway newspapers that most communities seem to have, or check the auction classified section of your daily paper. You can also ask your local antiques dealer if there is an area publication that lists auctions. If I'm in a strange town and have no idea what the auction story is, I use the yellow pages, call any auctioneer listed, and ask about upcoming local events.

Nationally, the Maine Antique Digest and the Newtown Bee, have the most comprehensive listings. (See Chapter Twenty.)

Truly impassioned collectors may want to think about subscribing to a search service. These computer services will let you know, via fax, e-mail, or even regular mail, if the particular items you're looking for will be coming up in an auction.

Here's how it works at Thesaurus, a Manhattan-

Ten Important Things to Do Before You Bid at an Auction

1. Register your name and address and get your paddle and/or bidding number as soon as you arrive. The lines get long right before the auction begins, and you'll want plenty of time to inspect the sale items.

2. Find out what kind of credit arrangements you can make at this time. Sotheby's sometimes lets its big spenders pay up a few months later, but smaller auctions usually want their money on the spot. Some will accept checks with proper identification, and a few now are willing to take credit cards.

3. Ask the auction staff how fast the auctioneer generally sells. The pace usually is from sixty to one hundred lots per hour. If you know in advance that this auctioneer sells at a rapid pace, you'll be able to figure out roughly when the items you are interested in will be coming up for sale.

4. If you think you might be buying something you won't be able to take home in your car, investigate what kind of shipping arrangements you can make or how long you would have to collect your merchandise after the auction ends. Some sales require immediate removal; others may give you as long as a week.

5. Make sure you get a catalog or lot list before you begin to check out merchandise. You'll need it to help you take notes. When you get the list, ask if any particular items will be sold at specific times. Sometimes auctioneers like to schedule the showstoppers at particular points during the auction to create excitement or accommodate a big spender.

6. Find out how long the auction is expected to last. Most auction houses can correctly estimate the length of the sale, and this is useful to know in advance, especially if you find out that the items you're most interested in buying aren't going to come up until midnight. Usually, auctioneers schedule the least important items in the very beginning, to allow latecomers time to arrive without feeling as though they've lost out too seriously. They also like to leave the rougher and less expensive or desirable items until the very last.

7. Find a seat that you're going to be comfortable with and reserve it. Usually at smaller auctions, you can save a seat simply by taping your name to it. Find a seat that's close enough to the auctioneer so that you can comfortably see what's happening, but not so close that you can't watch others bidding in front of you. A lot of dealers almost never sit down, but watch and wander from side to side, which is exhausting if the auction runs for the whole day.

8. Look at everything thoroughly in advance, using a flashlight to check behind and under furniture or inside drawers and doors. If there are box lots with a number of items jumbled together in a cardboard box, spend some time checking them out. Often, the real treasures are down at the bottom. (Sometimes dealers do this hoping no one else will notice the one valuable piece in the lot if it's buried deep enough.) If you're going to bid on a tablecloth or quilt, open it up fully to see what it is like all over. If you're looking at a carpet, check the back as well as the front. Check glassware for age and maker by inspecting the bottom; check vases or glasses for dings and cracks by running your finger over the edges. Look in, through, up, over, under, and behind everything and take notes as you go.

9. As you're making your inspection, this is the time to chat with others who are doing the same thing. It's especially important if you're not familiar with the auction house or area. Find out what the people around you think about the auction house itself, prices that these auctions bring, and anything else you can think of.

10. Make a restroom pit stop before the auction starts. It is a law of nature that you will be in the restroom when a lot you want comes up if you don't. Also, lines tend to be long.

based search service that has just opened in this country but has been operating successfully in Europe for ten years. You let the company know what kinds of antiques and collectibles you're looking for. You can limit your requests to one very specific area such as eighteenth-century tools, for example, or you can ask the company to give you blanket coverage for many different items. Thesaurus works with more than six hundred auction houses in this country and around the world who submit their lists of auction items to the search company in advance of the date of sale. They, in turn, let you know when and where the item you may want to buy is going to be sold. The service is also useful as a price guide. After the auction the company will let you know what the items in your areas of interest actually sold for.

The cost for all this efficiency isn't cheap, but it's not out of sight either. Generally fees range from $150 to $500 a year, according to Flora Hanft, the company's marketing director. You can reach Thesaurus at 1-800-491-FIND (3463).

CHAPTER FOUR

Northeast Region

Pennsylvania, New Jersey, New York, Maryland, Delaware

PENNSYLVANIA

Southeastern Pennsylvania—Routes 222 and 272

The southeastern corner of Pennsylvania is a top destination dealers from every other part of the country try to reach. It is still, in spite of the depredations of generations of antiquers, filled with a wealth of exciting and interesting pieces.

Antiquing in one form or another has been a primary income source for the people in this part of Pennsylvania for more than thirty years. Today, the most popular selling forum here is the ubiquitous mall; along Routes 222 and 272, there are dozens of them with everything from a small group of dealers to vast arenas with as many as five hundred. Most are clustered near Adamstown, which is essentially Exit 21 on the Pennsylvania Turnpike.

Because mall contracts for booths tend to be short-lived, although some dealers do turn into permanent occupants, the merchandise changes constantly. If a mall's stock seems mundane once, don't automatically cross it off your list until you've checked it out several times over a period of years.

During the summer, a lot of these malls add outdoor markets. These can be more rewarding because the sellers aren't dealers; more often just hobby antiquers who just like to buy and sell occasionally.

There is no lack of information about this corner of Pennsylvania. Every mall seems to be equipped with a plethora of paper, including brochures, maps, cards, auction notices, and trade newspapers. Auctions are conducted all year but they flourish in the summer months when the tourist season is at its busiest.

Plan on spending at least a few days if you decide to explore this area; it's impossible to cover more quickly. A lot of dealers give themselves two weeks to cover all the shops and malls as well as the weekend flea markets and a few auctions.

If you do stay overnight and get the chance, try to have dinner once at Stoudt's Tavern in Womersburg, Pennsylvania, close to Adamstown. It's a small restaurant located in a somewhat undistinguished pre-

Revolutionary War building. It's not cheap, but it's worth it.

The malls don't all conform to the same schedule, so it's not easy to predict when they're all open. Some are open seven days, others five, and they all have shorter hours during the winter months. If you find a mall you particularly like, call first to make sure it will be open on the day you plan to be in the area.

Adamstown is located very conveniently for the hard-core shopper. It's between Reading, where all the manufacturers' outlet malls are located and Lancaster, with its Amish and Mennonite farmer's markets and crafts shops.

TO GET THERE: Exit 21 is easy to get to from New York City or Philadelphia. Just take the Pennsylvania Turnpike and follow the signs. You'll see antiques malls as you exit.

FOR MORE INFORMATION: For a map or other information about this particular antiques area, write to the Exit 21 Tourist Association, P.O. Box 457R, Adamstown, PA, 19501

Renningers

Renningers, although it's part of the Route 222 group of antiques malls, really is in a class of its own. There are now two separate Renningers locations, each operating on a different day on the weekend, so if you want to check out both, you'll have to stay overnight.

The original Renningers is in Adamstown, just a short drive from Exit 21. Open on Sundays only, it has both indoor and outdoor selling spaces. The 375 indoor spaces are usually rented to regulars, while more transient dealers sell from the three hundred outdoor spaces available if the weather permits.

Shupp's Grove

This is one of the oldest outdoor flea markets in the southeastern Pennsylvania area and a lot of dealers know about it, though it doesn't seem to be as familiar to tourists.

It started in 1962 when a local antiques dealer began to operate a Sunday morning flea market in a grove of trees that had been a popular site for gospel revival meetings, country western shows, and picnics. At this time, most of the surrounding shops and markets didn't bother with antiques, so Shupp's Grove had the market to itself. Success was so quick that it spurred the development of many of the surrounding flea markets and malls.

Shupp's Grove is still the place bargain-hunting dealers hit first when they comb this area. It opens in April and operates, no matter what the weather, every weekend thereafter until the end of October. There are some special "extravaganzas"—three-day weekends when a lot more dealers participate. At these, there is an early buying period from 5 to 9 P.M. the evening before the weekend sale begins.

Shupp's Grove is one of the most pleasant markets in this area, because the trees make it cool and shady and the atmosphere is calm as a result. The management provides food stands that serve reasonably priced snacks and good coffee, and there are plenty of restrooms, even water bowls for pets.

TO GET THERE: Exit 21 off the Turnpike, turn right on Route 272 North, then right on Route 897 South. The Grove is three-quarters of a mile on the left.

FOR MORE INFORMATION: Write for brochures and schedules to: P.O. Box 892, Adamstown, PA, 19501

Stoudt's Antique Mall

Back in the late sixties, a restaurateur named Ed Stoudt took over the food concession at Shupp's Grove. He was an antiques collector himself and it wasn't long before he decided to open the basement of his Black Angus Restaurant as an indoor antiques market. That was 1971, and now the Antiques Mall that has grown around the original restaurant is a sprawling complex of indoor antiques booths, outdoor pavilions, a brewery, and individual antiques shops, crafts stores and artists' homes, and studios.

Indoors, the Clock Tower market is open fifty-two weeks a year, although it is closed mid-week on Tuesdays and Wednesdays. Outside, dealers set up for the Sunday market at about 5 A.M. and are ready to sell by 6 A.M. Because the three pavilions are covered, dealers appear every weekend from May through November. In the indoor buildings adjacent to the pavilions, other dealers maintain booths as well. All together about 800 dealers are on hand every Sunday during much of the year.

TO GET THERE: Stoudt's is about a half mile north of Renningers on Route 272 in Adamstown.
FOR MORE INFORMATION: Telephone 1-717-484-2757.

The second Renningers is in Kutztown, a few miles away on Route 22. The market is actually on Noble Street, one block south of Main Street. You'll see the signs. It's open only on Saturdays and has two hundred indoor booths and 125 outside ones. The adjacent farmer's market offers fresh produce, much of it raised on nearby Amish or Mennonite farms.

Expect to find the best buys by flashlight. The dealers are all out and around as the sellers start to set up just before dawn. The sellers themselves may be dealers or novices and prices range anywhere from a dollar or two for an embroidered baby's cap to thousands for a Tiffany-style leaded glass shade lamp. Adamstown seems to attract the higher-end dealers.

Renningers also does a number of annual special events. The Kutztown location hosts "extravaganzas" three times a year, usually on the last Thursday,

Friday, and Saturday in April, June, and September. These huge shows attract twelve hundred dealers from forty-two states, and this time you have to pay to get in. Early admission when dealers are setting up is $40 per car, for one to four people, on Thursdays. Friday's admission is $5 and Saturday's, $3.

There's also a Mid-Winter Classic show that is held indoors at the Valley Forge Convention Center in King of Prussia, PA, Exit 24 of the Turnpike. This show is always on a weekend in February.

Renningers operates very efficiently and, recognizing the value of publicity, its office is prepared to inundate you in paper if you like. Both locations offer a vast number of flyers, pamphlets, brochures, and free copies of the *Renningers Antique Guide,* a trade newspaper.

TO GET THERE: Exit 21 of the Pennsylvania Turnpike. **FOR MORE INFORMATION:** Write to Renningers, 27 Bensinger Drive, Schuykill Haven, PA 17971 or telephone 1-717-385-0414 Monday through Thursday.

Antique Complex of Fleetwood

Mom and Pop operations are the real life blood of the antiques business, with many couples going into business in mid-life, or even after retirement. Fleetwood Antiques is one of them, but now it encompasses a second generation in the same family.

Close to the heart of Pennsylvania's Adamstown cluster of antiques shops and malls on Route 222, the complex is actually located just south of the small town of Moselem Springs. The first building, now named Complex I, was started by Elaine and Jerry Arak in 1986.

Now one huge barn and a series of smaller buildings hold hundreds of reasonably priced antiques. A lot of the stock is unusual; the Araks also do a lot of prop rentals for theatrical productions.

Complex II, a half mile farther down the road, is where the second generation takes over. The Araks' son, Jack, and his wife, Sherry, manage this annex to the main store, along with a summertime outdoor flea market that's open on weekends from April through October.

On the third Saturday of every month, from June to October, the Araks conduct what they call a country tailgate auction. Anyone can bring merchandise to this auction and have it sold off the back of their vehicle on the spot. The Araks take a small percentage as a fee.

Fleetwood also hosts a number of special events that include everything from charity auctions to vintage car shows.

TO GET THERE: Follow Route 222 from Adamstown to Moselem Springs. Both locations are directly on the road.

FOR MORE INFORMATION: Write to Antique Complex of Fleetwood, Route 222, Fleetwood, PA, 19522 or telephone 1-619-944-0707.

NEW JERSEY

Lambertville

This antiques shops-filled town is located directly opposite the equally antiques shops-filled town of New Hope, Pennsylvania, just across the Delaware River. There is one important difference: although New Hope's shops are wonderful and filled with interesting and high quality antiques, Lambertville's prices in general are lower for the same things.

Dozens of individual and multi-dealer shops. Check Union Street, Bridge Street, Corkyell Street, Lambert Lane and Church Street.

TO GET THERE: The town is about a 45-minute drive from Philadelphia, and about 90 minutes from New York City. Take Interstate 95 to Route 29 North, which goes through Lambertville.

FOR MORE INFORMATION: Telephone 609-397-0055

Lambertville and Golden Nugget Antique Markets

The real bargains in Lambertville are just a mile

outside of town, heading south on Route 29, where two large flea markets operate alongside the road.

Both the Lambertville Antique Market and the Golden Nugget are located on the same side of the street and it's often difficult to tell where one ends and the other begins, because the several hundred outside tables are so close together. Each of these markets also offers indoor selling spaces where less transient dealers have set up shop. The Golden Nugget is open on Wednesdays, Saturdays, and Sundays, while the Lambertville Market operates Wednesday through Sunday, although days may vary for indoor and outdoor spaces.

Both markets also charge more to vendors on the weekends, so the best day to shop at Lambertville is probably Wednesday, because many antiques shops close on Wednesday in the area and a lot of dealers both buy and sell here then. The markets are open year-round and the action begins at daybreak as everyone unloads. Outdoor vendors are already packing up by noon, but the indoor dealers stay open until four or five.

TO GET THERE: The markets are located one mile south of Lambertville on Route 29, or 7 miles north from the Interstate 95 exit.

FOR MORE INFORMATION: Lambertville Antique Market, 1-609-397-0456 or Golden Nugget Antique Market, 1-609-397-0811.

Mullica Hill

This was one of those small, anonymous towns that could easily have faded into complete obscurity when the only important business closed back in the early seventies.

The town did, however, have one really enduring asset—a main street lined with exquisite, small Early American homes, many of them dating back to the eighteenth century. So when the old grist mill was revived as an antique shop and then expanded into a mall, it attracted more people who enjoyed antiques, and they in turn restored the Main Street homes and began to turn some of them into shops.

There are now more than one hundred dealers living in this community. The two malls—the Yellow Garage and the Old Mill, have eighty-five booths between them. Prices are surprisingly low, and as a result, the town has become a regular stop for Philadelphia dealers.

Some of the remaining historic houses have become bed-and-breakfasts for antiquers who want to stay overnight and check everything out.

Mullica Hill has a very active merchants' association that makes sure there are events to attract antiquers year-round. In the spring, there's usually a "mile-long" sale in which all the dealers participate. There are also spring and fall open houses, summer art shows and a garden party, an August doll show, and at Christmas, celebrations and house tours.

TO GET THERE: From the New Jersey Turnpike take the Swedesboro exit, Route 322, east to Mullica Hill.
FOR MORE INFORMATION: The Mullica Hill Merchants' Association, Box 235, Mullica Hill, NJ, 08062 will send a brochure, map, and description of upcoming events. Telephone 1-609-881-6800.

Atlantique City

This show in Atlantic City calls itself "the big one" and that's not an exaggeration. Twice a year, on a Saturday and Sunday in March and October, the Atlantic City Convention Center and the Miss America Auditorium on the Boardwalk host twelve hundred dealers who seem to have in aggregate every kind of antique you can think of. Dealers come from forty-four states, and from Canada, Great Britain, Europe, and Asia. The show is so vast it covers seven-and-a-half acres and twelve miles of indoor pathways.

Saturday admission is $15; Sunday admission $10; two-day ticket, $22.

TO GET THERE: East from Philadelphia, take the Atlantic City Expressway; from New York City, south on the Garden State Parkway. Follow Convention Center signs.
FOR MORE INFORMATION: For early admission tickets, airline and hotel discounts, telephone 1-800-526-2724.

NEW YORK

26th Street & Sixth Avenue Markets

It may seem difficult to believe that some of the best antique buys around can be found in the heart of Manhattan, but it's true. Dealers from at least six surrounding states flock to this part of the city to join in a popular Saturday and Sunday ritual for antiques lovers.

This is another market area that seems to just grow and grow. It began in one outdoor parking lot that was virtually empty on weekends, when most of the area's normal weekday businesses were closed. Then it expanded until the original market, the Annex Antiques Outdoor Fair and Flea Market, grew to fill lots from 24th Street to 27th Street on Sixth Avenue. (Actually, the street is named Avenue of the Americas, but nobody pays any attention to the official name.)

Across from the Annex is The Garage, a two-story weekend market in an indoor garage with more than one hundred dealers on West 25th Street between Sixth and Seventh Avenues. There are also a couple of permanent indoor antiques buildings in the area. And along the perimeter of the outdoor lots are a lot of extracurricular sales from trucks or on the sidewalk.

Although the market opens officially at 8:00 A.M., most of the serious hunting is done earlier when people show up before dawn with flashlights to "help" the dealers unload. Admission fees are minimal; some lots are free while others charge $1.

Note: You're on your own when it comes to telling the true from the false at any market, but these outdoor parking lot shows don't seem to have as much reproduction material as many malls I've checked.

The best times to go to these markets are in the spring and fall. They operate almost year-round, as long as the weather is tolerable, but in the summer, a lot of the dealers who would come here don't show up because they're out in the country doing shows there.

TO GET THERE: Subway or bus to 23rd Street and Sixth Avenue; walk uptown toward the markets.

FOR MORE INFORMATION: Chelsea Antiques Building, Telephone, 1-212-929-0909

Tepper Galleries

Also located in Manhattan, this long established auction house may not be quite as fancy as Sotheby's but it has some very attractive merchandise including fine antiques and collectibles. Tepper specializes in selling out estates, so the merchandise is always eclectic, although they don't auction the yard sale or flea market type of merchandise. They do sell furniture, china, lamps, carpets, art work and almost any kind of decorative accessory. Occasionally, perhaps every two months or so, a special auction of jewelry or art is scheduled.

Dealers do buy here, and the best time to find good values at Tepper is during the summer when many of the area dealers are out of town selling at shows or summer markets.

The auctions are always on Saturdays, starting at 10 A.M. and they usually end about 8 P.M. You can inspect the sale merchandise the Friday before from 9 A.M. to 7 P.M.

TO GET THERE: Located at 110 East 25th Street, New York, NY

FOR MORE INFORMATION: Telephone 1-212-673-3686.

Madison-Bouckville Antiques Show

This show, which attracts about one thousand dealers to an upstate New York cornfield once a year, always on the third weekend in August, is one of the most interesting in the country. Until recently, it was regarded strictly as a dealer's show, a place to hunt for diamonds in the rough; most of the people who flocked to this unobtrusive spot on Route 20 in central New York were in the antiques trade in one way or another. Collectors are drawn to it now, but it's still a place to find great buys. The show was organized twenty-five years ago, as a way for local merchants to draw business back to Route 20, which was becoming a backwater after the New

York State Thruway began to draw the majority of travelers. The show itself covers thirty acres but a lot of independent dealers and area residents set up their own offshoots along the road nearby.

TO GET THERE: Take Interstate 90 to Utica, then south to Route 20 and west. Look for signs.

FOR MORE INFORMATION: Write to Madison-Bouckville Management, P.O. Box 97, Hamilton, NY, 13346 or telephone 1-313-824-2462 for a free show program and information packet.

Hudson Valley

If you follow the Hudson River from New York City north all the way to Albany, as early traders used to do, you will find rich troves of antiques along the way. Check out the city of Hudson itself, which is replete with group and individual shops. Don't forget Rhinebeck, (on New York's Route 9) which has a very interesting group shop behind the Beckman Arms and Red Hook, where a lot of dealers congregate.

TO GET THERE: Hudson is two-and-a-half hours from New York City on the New York State Thruway, Exit 21.

Copake Country Auction

This is a real dealers' auction; it's the kind of place that attracts area shopowners regularly because the quality of the merchandise is always good. For example, a recent auction included the entire contents of a small museum that had closed. Auctions are held on average of about twice a month and the size of the sale does vary. There is a 10% buyer's premium.

TO GET THERE: Taconic State Parkway to Route 23 east to Hillsdale, then Route 22 to Copake. The auction house is directly on Route 22 as you enter the town.

FOR MORE INFORMATION: Write to Box H, Route 22, Copake, NY 12516 or telephone: 1-518-329-1142

The Rhinebeck Antiques Fair

It's only held twice a year—in May and then again in October—but this show is one that dealers in the New York area always try to catch because of the quality. There are 190 dealers showing wares from $25 to $25,000 according to Jim Barton, who along with Bill Walters organizes the semi-annual show. Indoors, it's held at the Dutchess County Fairgrounds on Saturday and Sunday from 11 A.M. to 5 P.M. both days. There is no early admission at all, so everyone gets the same chance to buy. Admission is $6.

TO GET THERE: Exit 19 off the New York State Thruway, Kingston-Rhinecliff Bridge to 9G, south to Route 9 and south one mile.

FOR MORE INFORMATION: P.O. Box 310, Red Hook, NY 12571, or telephone 1-914-758-6186.

Hyde Park Antiques Center

A 55-dealer, two-story mall, this 10,000 sq. ft. center has everything from fine eighteenth- and nineteenth-century furniture to silver, porcelain, buttons, toys, and jewelry. The merchandise is of good quality. Sixty percent of the sales are to dealers.

The center has been located in this building, originally an 18th century stage coach stop, for 16 years. For the past three years, it has been voted the best antiques shop in Dutchess County by local area newspapers and magazines.

TO GET THERE: The Antiques center is located halfway between the Roosevelt Museum and the Vanderbilt Museum on Albany Post Road. Take Route 9 north to reach Hyde Park.

FOR MORE INFORMATION: Hyde Park Antiques Center, 544 Albany Post Road, Hyde Park, NY 12538, or telephone 1-914-229-8200.

Hudson

This small, pleasant Hudson River town has dozens of antiques dealers in forty stores, most of them located on Warren Street. The range of antiques is amazing; prices are good, too.

All the shops are open year-round, but hours and days vary. Most close on Wednesdays.

TO GET THERE: Hudson is two hours north of New York City. Take the New York State Thruway or the Taconic Parkway to the Hudson exits.

FOR MORE INFORMATION: Telephone the Hudson Antique Center, 1-518-828-9920, or contact the Columbia County Chamber of Commerce, 507 Warren Street, Hudson, NY 12534, 1-518-828-4417

Eastern Long Island

Walt Whitman called Long Island a fish with its head pointing toward New York City and its tail flipping out into the Atlantic Ocean. That "tail" has become a focal point for antiquers who travel out to the eastern end of the island, especially during the summer.

The South Fork of this tail is the fashionable Hamptons area, and it is chock-full of antiques shops. Like many resort communities, rents aren't cheap and as a result, prices tend to be high. Good buys, however, are available at Liza Werner's Sage Street Antiques in Sag Harbor, where there's always a line waiting to get in on Saturdays and Sundays, at Morgan MacWhinnie's shop complex at 1411 North Sea Road in Southampton, and at Ruby Beets

Antiques on Route 27 just east of Bridgehampton. There are antique shows in the area almost every weekend during the summer.

Prices get much better when you drive over to the North Fork. Because this area, filled with vineyards and farmer's markets, is not yet as developed as the Hamptons, prices for everything, including antiques, are much lower. Check out Jan Davis Antiques on Route 25, near Mattituck. Greenport and Orient, two of the easternmost towns on the North Fork, have interesting quality shops.

TO GET THERE: Long Island Expressway from New York City to Exits 70, 71 and 72. Follow signs for Montauk to the South Fork; follow signs for Orient and Greenport for the North Fork.

FOR MORE INFORMATION: Mongan MacWhinnie, 1-516-283-3366; Sage Street Antiques, 1-516-725-4036; Ruby Beets, 1-516-537-2802.

MARYLAND

Olsen's, Inc.

Roger Olsen, along with his wife, Carolyn, has been operating their antique business since 1947, and has been in this same Maryland location for almost 35 years. The store is memorable because the entire ceiling is covered with 450 chairs in an unusual hanging display. Olsen's also has about 250 hanging chandeliers at any given time, and, as Olsen says, "about umpteen thousand pieces of everything." Prices range, he adds, from $1 to $3,000. The store is open from 9 to 5 Wednesday through Saturday, 1 to 5 on Sundays year-round.

TO GET THERE: Olsen's is in Westover, Maryland, on the Eastern Shore, close to the Virginia border, on US Route 13.

FOR MORE INFORMATION: Write to Olsen's, Inc., at 31648 Curtis Chapel Road, Westover, Maryland, 21871

Antique Mall in the Shops at Ellicott Mills

This former mill town on the outskirts of Baltimore now hosts not only this new antiques shop, with more than 100 dealers, but many others as well. Multi-dealer malls, incidentally, are often called "emporiums" in Maryland and Delaware.

You should also check out Taylor's nearby on Main Street and The Depot, just a few steps off Main Street.

In addition, there are dozens of small independent shops in this quaint and interesting little town. Ask for directions at the larger malls.

TO GET THERE: Ellicott City is about 10 minutes from the center of Baltimore and about 30 minutes from

Washington, D.C. From Baltimore, take Highway 103 from Interstate 70. From D.C., take Interstate 95 north to MD Route 100 north.

FOR MORE INFORMATION: Write to 8307 Main Street, Ellicott City, MD 21043, or telephone 1-410-461-8700.

Frederick, Maryland

Located in the western part of the state, close to the Virginia border, Frederick is actually only a 45-minute drive from Baltimore. It's worth the trip because the entire town has become one vast antiques complex, with at least 1,000 dealers in the immediate area, many of them in the huge malls that dominate the antiques landscape here.

The town itself is pleasantly historic and in addition to the many malls that dot the area, has dozens of small independent antiques shops lining the streets of the downtown historic district.

Among the largest malls are The Emporium, with 130 dealers, Frederick's Best, with close to 200 dealers, the Antique Station, with about 110 dealers, Old Glory, also with more than 100 dealers and Baker's Row Antique Marketplace, with at least another 100. Add up the smaller malls and the shops, and you have an antiques Mecca where prices are considerably lower than they would be if you were to shop a little closer to metropolitan Washington, D.C. and Baltimore.

The town has made a major effort to support the

antiques trade here; there are dozens of restaurants and the entire downtown area has been renovated carefully to preserve the historic character and look of the town.

TO GET THERE: Frederick can be reached directly from Interstate 70. If you get off at the Frederick Historic District exit, which is marked, you will be in downtown Frederick almost immediately. All the antiques shops are loaded with maps to let you know where everyone else is located. A few of the shops and malls are open seven days; most however are closed on Wednesdays.

FOR MORE INFORMATION: The Emporium at Creekside, 112 East Patrick Street. Telephone 1-301-662-7099. Old Glory Antique Mall, 5862 Urbana Pike. Telephone 1-301-662-9173. Baker's Row Antique Marketplace, 125 Carroll Street. Telephone 1-301-662-4853.

DELAWARE

Antique Village at Red Mill

Lewes, a small town on the eastern Delaware shore, attracts a lot of summer visitors because of its proximity to the beaches. As a result, the town is becoming another antique center that is growing rapidly with several new malls, or emporiums, opening during the past year. There are now close to 200 dealers in Lewes, some in the town's two malls, and others operating independently.

TO GET THERE: Take US Route 13 south from Wilmington to Route 113. Go south on 113 to State Route 1. Follow Route Interstate 1, which follows the coastline, to Route 9. Or take the ferry from Cape May, NJ.

FOR MORE INFORMATION: Antique Village at Red Mill, 321 Highway One, Lewes, Delaware 19958 or telephone 1-302-644-0842.

Bargain Bill's Antique and Flea Market

A huge, bustling flea market that many coastal area dealers use as a primary source to stock their shops is located in western Delaware at the southern corner of the state. The market has approximately 300 indoor booths where a lot of antiques dealers have set up permanent selling locations. Outside, the more fluid dealer population operates from an additional 200 tables. The market is open Fridays, Saturdays and Sundays year-round.

TO GET THERE: US Route 13, south from Dover, Delaware to Route 9. The market is located at the junction of the two roads.

FOR MORE INFORMATION: Write Bargain Bill's, RD 4,

Box 547, Laurel, Delaware 19956, or telephone 1-302-875-2478.

ADDENDUM: Don't skip the town of Laurel when you get to the flea market. Laurel has at least a half-dozen multi-dealer shops with dozens of dealers operating through them. Check out the Delaware Avenue Antique Emporium, which has just expanded to add Parker's Place, another mall with a backyard barn filled with primitives.

CHAPTER FIVE

DEALER HABITATS

Shops, Malls, Shows, and Flea Markets

Dealers like to gather in groups, and that's not because they're giving in to some atavistic tribal urge. Antique shops are a little like peanuts; the more you eat, the more you want, and dealers know that a town with, say, a dozen shops, will attract a lot more people every day than will one small store, no matter how fabulous.

Whether you're buying from a dealer in an individually owned store, an antique co-op or mall, a flea market or show, you aren't competing quite as directly as you would during an auction, but you can expect a little tug-of-war over price.

This time, on his or her own selling turf, the dealer definitely has the home team advantage. Here, the dealer's already done the hardest part— finding the merchandise, fluffing it up a little bit, and putting it on display. Obviously, you're no longer going to be able to expect a rock-bottom price because the dealer not only has to recoup the initial investment along with expenses but wants to make a profit as well.

However, as the customer, you actually have something else working in your favor. Most antiques dealers are not selling their wares because they just love to sell. If that were the case, they'd be selling cars or computers or real estate where the money's a whole lot better. They're selling antiques instead because they love to *buy* antiques. For a lot of dealers, selling is merely the mechanism that provides the money to go out and buy, buy, buy some more.

So, if the dealer you encounter is anxious to scratch that buying itch, it suddenly is going to be a whole lot easier for you to negotiate a better price.

Everyone who sells antiques, no matter what the venue, expects a little wheeling and dealing over the price. It's been my experience that in the most expensive stores, prices often seem to be the most inflexible. In less formal surroundings, and particularly at flea markets, you have a lot of negotiating room.

In some antiques malls and co-ops, where dealers don't have to be in regular attendance at booths or stalls, discounts are written in code on the price tags. You'll often see a price of $25, lets say, with a notation in the opposite corner that indicates the seller will accept a ten-percent discount. Sometimes these discount percentages are written alphabetically, so that ten percent is an "A," fifteen percent a "B," and so on, and sometimes the price is simply reduced by a dollar figure. Most of the codes are fairly easy to figure out. Just look at a number of price tags in several different booths and you'll probably be able to work out what the discount would be. If the code seems a little complex, take a few things to the checkout counter and ask what the discounted price might be. When you look back at the tag, you'll see how the discount was calculated.

Antique co-ops and malls may not be very anxious to talk about any deeper discounts when the actual seller is not present. However, if you're insistent, you may be able to wheedle the checkout people into calling the absent dealer at home for further negotiations. Obviously this isn't worth anybody's time if you're talking about a couple of dollars. However, if you're buying a large piece of furniture or an expensive bit of glassware, making the effort to increase the discount is worth the try.

How insistent can you be? Well, bargaining is practically an art form in and of itself that requires a moment-by-moment assessment of the situation, so there are no hard-and-fast rules. Most dealers almost always build a ten-percent discount into their asking prices, so you can reasonably expect to ask for this reduction everywhere without getting a frosty glare. On a bad day, when sales are slow, you might be able to get fifteen or as much as twenty percent off.

When you go a whole lot further than that, you head into very risky terrain because the closer you get to fifty percent, the closer you usually are to the dealer's actual cost. In clothing, jewelry, souvenirs, and even eyeglasses, fifty percent discounts are common even though they may be based on an inflated price in the first place. You don't see a lot of this kind of artificial discounting in the antiques world, probably because most customers have seen enough price guides to get a reasonable idea of what prices are in any given category.

Aggressive browbeating in an attempt to widen that discount window almost never works, as a customer in Bobby Jones' East Hampton antiques shop learned the day he grabbed Bobby's arm and tried to force Bobby's fingers around six one-hundred dollar bills he'd been futility offering for a set of chairs priced at $1,000. As the customer grabbed Bobby he said, "Now, this is what we're going to do! You're going to take this money and I'm going to take these chairs!"

Bobby said, "No, this is what *I'm* going to do . . ." and in short order, everyone on East Hampton's very posh and proper Newtown Lane got to watch the customer running like crazy up the street, Bobby hard on his heels, holding one of the chairs above his head and telling the customer exactly what he intended to do with it when he caught him.

The point is, of course, that antiques dealers are a pretty independent lot and will bristle if pushed too hard. You can get a whole lot farther by admiring a dealer's acumen and taste and acknowledging quality and value, than you ever will by trying to manipulate the price downward.

It's almost worth the expense of a trip to London to see a couple of English antiques enthusiasts bargain back and forth over price. It's done with such good manners and careful verbal tugging and pulling that it's practically theater. And when it's all over, both parties have what they wanted out of the deal but the amenities of civilized conduct have been preserved.

You don't want to make yourself vulnerable, though, when you see something that enchants you. Once, I walked into a store and saw a cobalt blue footed goblet that matched a partial set I'd had for years. Well, I didn't have the good sense to keep my mouth shut. I burbled all over about what luck it was to finally find one that would complete my set and of course, the dealer was listening with a tiny triumphant smile. There was no way to bargain after that.

I usually don't even ask for a price on the piece I'm most interested in getting from a dealer when I first begin to negotiate. Instead, I'll ask about, discuss, pause, reconsider, and discuss again two or three other things before trying a sort of sideways

"Oh well, by the way, since I'm here anyway, what about that old chair . . ." approach.

Usually, flea markets offer the best deals, shows the most interesting variety, and malls the widest range, but there are some built-in bargains in almost every antiques shop. That's because dealers often gravitate after a while to a few areas of interest and become extremely knowledgeable about them. However, it's just impossible for a dealer to have an encyclopedic store of information about everything. With a little luck, you can take advantage of those gaps.

A few years ago I bought, and still own, a Fremont Indian grindstone set. It came from anther dealer who has a shop in Utah. Although that's certainly Indian territory, she preferred frou-frou things and her store was filled with really wonderful dolls and delicate glassware. The grindstone had come in as a consignment piece and didn't interest her, so she priced it at $55. With my dealer discount, it went down to $44. The value? Try adding a zero, at least, to the price I paid.

In another store, you might find the dealer knows everything there is to know about Indian blankets, even though the store's located in a city in the East, but could care less about Depression-era glass and sells it for a song.

Sometimes pricing is keyed to local preferences. For a while in the East, oak furniture was much despised, and dealers who had bought at auction and then discovered oak underneath a thick coat of paint would moan and wail because they'd hoped to find pine. Now, of course, oak is hot everywhere.

However, there are still parts of the country where certain things sell well and others simply don't. Milk glass, for example, is popular in Baltimore, I'm told, but it doesn't generate much interest in other parts of the Northeast. Clear glass, on the other hand, draws good response in the Northeast but languishes on store shelves in the West, no matter how old and beautiful, unless it's been sunweathered to purple.

When you walk into a shop that's located in an expensive part of town, one of those attractive boutique areas filled with wonderful restaurants and interesting stores, remember that you're paying for all that ambience. Dealers' prices have to reflect the cost of overhead, and when rent is expensive, so are the antiques. That's why you'll usually find the better antiques bargains in the grungier parts of town, or off the beaten path in rural areas.

Antiques malls have become the best way for a lot of dealers to combat the cost of doing business. Usually, space rental prices in malls are fairly low. The dealers don't have to stand the expense of hiring employees either, although some malls do expect their tenants to pitch in as part of the sales staff for a few days every week or month.

You'd think this kind of cost-effective salesmanship would automatically mean that mall prices would always be low, really low, but that's not necessarily true. Logic is not a watchword of the antiques world. But in general, you'll find some of the better bargains in the malls.

If they have a drawback, it's that they often reflect that old saying: "birds of a feather flock together." If one dealer in a mall really loves those black velvet Elvis paintings or the small tufted carpets woven with the pictures of dogs playing cards, chances are that other dealers with similar taste will gravitate to the same location. And since rents in malls are usually calculated on the basis of square footage, the tendency is for dealers to cram their small stalls or booths with as much stuff as possible, leading to eye-glazing, mind-numbing clutter as a result.

Sometimes the infighting can be so fierce that it affects the entire selling atmosphere. Once I walked into a mall in Pennsylvania where some sort of palace revolution seemed to be in progress. On all three levels, groups of dealers had gathered into warring factions that alternately glared and muttered. I don't think a lot of merchandise left the building that day because the dealers were so focused on their internal warfare that they forgot customers were coming and going.

Usually these kinds of battles break out because one dealer feels another is deliberately sabotaging sales, or undercutting the other members of the co-operative in some way. I have been in malls where dealers working on their selling days have tried to convince me to abandon the item I'm about to purchase, claiming they can get me a better version at a cheaper price privately outside the store.

For exactly this reason, the better malls try to avoid having dealers handle the actual sales. They may become floorwalkers or general help, but there is a professional staff of mangers to take care of the actual transactions.

The only way to make an end run around a mall salesperson who is not being helpful for one reason or another is to write down the booth number or dealer number, the item number, and the location in the mall carefully and then contact the mall manager to see if you can rustle up a little more cooperation.

Particularly when the weather's good, a lot of mall dealers, and even those with independent stores, head out on the weekends to sell at shows or flea markets.

Flea markets can be a lot of fun. As the last bastion of the original itinerant peddler who roamed the countryside selling his wares, the flea market is, by definition, the perfect spot for any dealer who wants to limit overhead to almost nothing.

The dealers who sell at flea markets have to pay only a few dollars for a space or table and don't need to invest in any other business expense except, perhaps, a canopy or umbrella, and gas for the truck or van to get them there. Usually vendors at flea markets don't have to commit themselves to more than one weekend at a time, although some certainly do. The result is that merchandise is always changing as vendors come and go, making the chances of finding a truly wonderful treasure much higher than they'd be at a less fluid sales venue.

When you get to a flea market, try to find out where the occasional dealers are located and go there right away. Usually, it's the least desirable part of the market, the section that is the longest distance from the parking lot, for instance, or in the direct hot sun rather than under the trees. This is always the place for the best buys. In Canton, Texas, for example, where there's a wonderful monthly flea market (see page 229) the newcomer's and occasional vendor's area is called "the glory hole" and it's the part of the market dealers sprint to first.

If you're serious about hunting for antiques at flea markets, you'd better plan on arriving about the time the sun comes up. This is when the dealers, flashlights in hand, will be checking out the vendors as they begin to offload and unpack. The market may not actually open for another hour or two, but in most, there are early buying opportunities. In the largest and most structured markets, early buyers have to pay an extra fee. In the smaller, more informal markets, the only requirement for early buyers is a willingness to stumble around in the dark.

You are strictly on your own when you buy at a market. If the owner tells you that the painting you like is a nineteenth-century reverse glass work, and you find out when you get home that it's just glass over a page from a calendar, there's not a lot you can do. Most flea market merchandise is sold "as is." If you are buying from an established dealer at a flea market, and the piece you're looking at has a very hefty price, try to get as much of a guarantee in writing as you can on the spot. You'll want to make sure you and the dealer both understand the return policy, if any, and the seller should be willing to give you either a business or home address and telephone number.

Flea markets are unpredictable by nature and that is also their only real drawback. Often, a flea market will become a ripe spot for antiques hunting, a place where you begin to routinely expect to find fantastic things. Then, suddenly, the antiques people stop bringing the things and the only good buys are on local vegetables. And a lot of outdoor flea markets are located in open fields which are, in turn, subject to the vagaries of the real estate market or changes in local zoning codes.

If you're going to spend a lot of time and effort getting to what seems to be a particularly promising market, always call in advance and make sure the market is actually going on that weekend, even if you feel you could bet money that it is. I know one dealer who drove for four hours to get to a market he was certain would always be there and found on arrival, an empty field and the beginnings of a foundation hole for a building.

Flea markets are the poor relations of the organized antiques shows, which can be very fancy indeed. The Winter Antiques Show in New York City, for example, is one of the city's most important society events; dealers come from all over the world to buy and sell incredibly exquisite treasures at prices that go up into the hundreds of thousands of dollars.

A lot of shows serve as fund-raisers for charities, and their opening hours are often cocktail parties or dinners at which patrons are prepared to part with substantial amounts of money.

The best shows "vet" their dealers, which means they make sure that all the dealers are selling merchandise that is exactly as it is represented to be. You have the right, when you buy from a dealer at an established show, to expect that the merchandise is genuine. If it's not, you do have recourse here. Talk to the show organizers; they will usually be more than helpful.

Because show organizers want to lure you through the door—almost all shows charge some form of admission—advertising usually emphasizes the upscale nature of the event and the quality of the merchandise. That may or may not be true. Some shows can be pretty sad affairs, with little to recommend them above your friendly outdoor flea market. Reputation is really what makes a show. If reliable dealers are associated with one, they will usually return again and again.

Because shows cost you money before you even buy anything, you should judge the value of one not just by what you've bought, but how interesting the total look of the show turned out to be. For your few dollars admission fee, you ought to see at least a few things that awe and amaze you. If it's all run-of-the-mill stuff, next time the show comes to town scratch it off your list.

Looking at antiques shows from the dealer's point of view, it's a really tough way to make a living. Some dealers actually do shows fifty-two weeks a year, traveling constantly, and seem to enjoy it. But consider the effort involved. The dealer has to load up a truck with merchandise, drive to the show's location, set up an attractive display of merchandise (and that usually means a fair amount of heavy lifting), sit around for a day or two or three being determinedly pleasant to prospective customers and eating junk food, and finally with varying degrees of satisfaction, depending upon how much has been sold, pack up and haul everything that's left back home, only to start the process all over again.

And for all this work, there are absolutely no guarantees to a dealer that as much as one thing will be sold. While shopkeepers or mall vendors can weather the vagaries of poor selling days, or seasons, show antiques dealers have only a few hours to make or break it.

There are some days when people, for inexplicable but apparently cosmic reasons, simply don't want to buy anything at all. Ask any antiques dealer and you will learn that there are times when the dealer could put a sign on all the merchandise that says "everything here free" and it still wouldn't leave the store because . . . well, who knows why, but believe me, it happens.

If that kind of cloud settles over a show, the dealer is done for. I know brilliant antiques dealers who've gone into good shows, set up wonderful exhibits, paid several hundred dollars for the privilege of doing so, and then sold less than $40 in an entire weekend.

How does all this affect you, the buyer? I've often read newspaper or magazine articles that suggest you can make a real killing at an antiques show by wandering in at the very end and lowballing the dealers. The theory is that dealers hate to pack the stuff up so much that they're willing to heavily discount their prices at the last minute.

I suppose it's possible that all the dealers I know just happen to be way too temperamental for that, but I think this last-minute effort to finagle an already weary dealer into a bottom-line price is always a mistake. You are liable to get nothing but some fairly choice language. If the dealer's done well at the show, he or she could care less about your attempts to garner a super buy. If the dealer's done badly, chances are better than average that the poor person is definitely depressed, probably surly, and certainly looking for a way to vent. Be warned.

What you should do if you want to dicker with a dealer a little more, is get the person's card, make a note on the back with the asking price, and then find out when a good time might be to call. You will get a better deal that way. I promise you.

Now, the very best show bargains will only be found at the very beginning. I realize all this early-bird-gets-the-worm stuff is getting a little tiresome, but most shows will offer early buying, at an additional price of course, and if you're seriously looking for something, grit your teeth and pay it. All the dealers are going to do it, so you might as well, too.

How to Tell if It's Genuine

Old Wood. Wood is organic; it changes and shrinks with age. As it grows old, particularly in soft woods, the grain will show stronger contrasts as cells of the softer sections begin to dry up and collapse. Because of the cellular changes, no wood construction stays exactly the same over time. It is also extremely susceptible to wear. Look on chairs for wear patterns on the rungs or rockers. On legs of tables, or nightstands, tip the piece up so you can inspect the base of the leg. There should be signs of wear on the bottom and in the last few inches of the leg.

Old Bureaus. The easiest way to check a bureau's age is by opening a drawer. (This applies to other furniture pieces with drawers, too.) At the side of the drawer, look closely at the dovetailing. If there are only a few joins, perhaps three or four, and they are not exactly alike, the bureau's really old—eighteenth or early-nineteenth century. If the dovetailing is a dot within a scallop, you can date the bureau exactly to the Civil War era. If the dovetailing is a multiple crenelated design with each cut exactly alike, chances are it is machine made and probably twentieth century. Also check the width of the drawer bottom. Earlier bureaus have thicker ones. Don't rule out a piece just because it has plywood. Plywood was in use in the nineteenth century.

Real Gold. Although it's usually marked with the karat strength—10, 12, 14, and less commonly 18 or 24—not all gold is stamped, especially if the piece has been custom-made by a jeweler. You can test the validity of a piece you think might be gold with a jeweler's testing kit, available inexpensively for $20 to $30 from a jewelry supply firm, or ask your local jeweler to get one for you.

Silver Versus Silverplate. Usually, but again not always, silverplate is stamped with the initials I.S. or E.N.P.S. It may also say "quadruple plate" or have the manufacturer's particular euphemism for plate stamped somewhere on the bottom.

Weights of plate silver do count when evaluating value. Sterling silver is often stamped "sterling," but if it comes from Europe or Mexico, it may be stamped 925 or 525 instead of the word sterling. Sterling doesn't shine up any better than plate.

Vaseline Glass. This luminous yellow translucent glass with a slight greenish tinge is highly prized by collectors; a piece of vaseline glass is going to be worth many more times the price of the same design in another color.

Naturally, this means that reproduction vaseline glass is creeping into the market. And, there are other yellow shades of glass that may be old, but they're not the distinctive vaseline, which was created by adding uranium to the molten glass. To verify vaseline glass, buy a small black light, also available inexpensively. When you shine it on the real thing, the glass gives off a distinctive fluorescent glow.

Alexandrite Glass. This is a real prize if you find it; one piece may be worth hundreds. Alexandrite is a gemstone that changes colors during day or night. It may change from red to green or pink to purple. Sometimes the changes will show in artificial vis à vis natural light, too. If you spot a piece of translucent glass and it seems to change color when you bring it indoors or outdoors, you may have stumbled upon a piece that's extremely valuable.

Amethyst Glass. This isn't even close to some of the other glass types in terms of value, but it's very collectible. Amethyst glass looks as though it's really black. But when you hold a piece up to direct light, either indoors or outdoors, you will see the purple color appear.

Ivory. A lot of old ivory is being properly sold, although most new ivory has been banned for some time. Ivory, too, is organic. As it ages, it tends to darken and sometimes will show hairline cracks. The quick test for ivory is to hold a match to it. If it's genuine, it won't burn easily. If it's bone masquerading as ivory, or plastic, which happens a lot, it will scorch.

CHAPTER SIX

MID-ATLANTIC REGION

North Carolina, South Carolina, Virginia, West Virginia, Washington, DC

NORTH CAROLINA

Metrolina Expo

North Carolina is, of course, better known for its new furniture manufacturing outlets than it is for antiques. But actually the state is a good place to look for Victorian furniture and folk art.

The Expo is the largest monthly market in the nation, with five thousand participating dealers. Not all of them show every month, but if you go to the Expo on the first and third weekends of each month, you will certainly be able to find buys.

The Expo has seventeen indoor buildings and fifteen tents, as well as twenty thousand free parking spaces for visitors. There are camping facilities available as well.

Three times a year, in April, June, and November, the Metrolina Expo hosts the "Great American Antiques Spectacular," when even more dealers converge here for these special shows. The length of the shows varies, but there are always sneak previews for early buying. Normal admission is $5 per day.

TO GET THERE: The Expo is five minutes north of downtown Charlotte; take Interstate 77 to Exit 16A, Sunset Road.

FOR MORE INFORMATION: Telephone 1-800-824-3770 or 1-704-596-4643.

Riverfront Antique Mall

This large antique mall, operated by the same people who run the Riverfront Mall in Ohio, has more than 300 dealers in an air-conditioned building close to North Carolina's furniture manufacturing area. Fine antiques along with a rough room.

TO GET THERE: This mall is 45 minutes away from both Charlotte and Winston-Salem in Statesville. Interstates 40 and 77 meet in Statesville.

FOR MORE INFORMATION: Write to 14411 Wilkesboro Road, Statesville, NC 28677, or telephone 1-800-856-2182.

SOUTH CAROLINA

Roumillat Antique Mall and Auction

Charleston is one of this country's loveliest cities, and a tourist delight. Not surprisingly, there are lots of antiques shops in the city. Downtown King Street is the mecca for people who love to wander through exquisite shops filled with stylish antiques, many European in origin. But away from these downtown shops, which are "fully priced," to use a local euphemism for expensive, are dozens of dealers with more eclectic merchandise and lower prices.

The Roumillat mall, with 60 dealers, also conducts a regular antiques auction, on the first and third Saturdays of the month, year-round, and always at 11 A.M. There are another four malls in Charleston, including the Grey Goose and Terrace Oaks, as well as dozens of independent dealer shops. The dealer population altogether—close to 500.

TO GET THERE: Interstate 95 from north or south to Interstate 26 southeast directly to Charleston.
FOR MORE INFORMATION: Ed Roumillat, 2241 Savannah Highway, Charleston, South Carolina 29414, or telephone 1-803-766-8899.

Columbia Antique Mall

The town of Columbia, although not as well known as Charleston to visitors from out of state, nevertheless has an active and growing population of antiques dealers that rivals Charleston's. There are at least 15 multi-dealer malls in Columbia and dozens of other individual shops. Most of them are clustered in the downtown area, along the banks of the Congaree River, both on the east and west sides of the stream.

The Columbia Mall is a one-story building with 25,000 sq. feet of space (35 dealers show here) and a wide range of unusual and colorful antiques. The mall is dotted with strange and fascinating objects, large and small, including a genuine gypsy caravan and an old-fashioned beer truck complete with wooden beer barrels.

TO GET THERE: Follow Interstate 26 right into Columbia's downtown area.

FOR MORE INFORMATION: Columbia Antique Mall, 602 Huger Street, Columbia, South Carolina 29201, or telephone 1-803-765-1484.

VIRGINIA

Hillsville

Tucked away in the mountainous southwestern corner of the state, this annual Labor Day weekend show draws 300,000 people to the town of 2,300 for the four days it's open. Two thousand vendors sell primarily antiques, as well as some gift items and crafts. Good primitives and folk art. This weekend market is so huge that all motels for 100 miles around are booked. If you go, make your reservations early.

TO GET THERE: Interstate 77 to Highway 58
FOR MORE INFORMATION: 1-540-728-5397 or write to: VFW Post 1115, 701 West Stuart Drive, Hillsville, VA 24343.

Antiques for the Home Show

This October show is actually located in Chantilly, Virginia, but it is considered one of Washington's favorite annual events because the dealers who are showing their antiques here display them in 150 room settings. The range of furniture, lighting, carpets and other decorative items runs from country to formal. Open Saturday and Sunday; admission, $5, is good for both days.

The show producers also do a well-regarded show at the Expo Center in April, as well as one in Arlington, Virginia in June and McLean, Virginia in November.

TO GET THERE: The show is at the Capital Expo Center near Dulles Airport on Route 28 at Willard Road, just south of Highway 50.
FOR MORE INFORMATION: Call Sha-Dor show manage-

ment at 1-301-738-1966 for a schedule of annual events, or write to P.O. Box 1400, Rockville, MD 20849-1400.

Shenandoah Antiques Expo

This semi-annual antiques show, in October and May attracts 200 indoor dealers along with at least another 250 who set up outside.

It's the nineteenth year that Stanford and Mary Ferguson and Martha and Ray Stokes, two couples who are also antiques dealers have produced this show in the valley of Virginia. East Coast dealers from Maine to Florida are presented, as are some from Canada and France.

Early admission buyers pay $10 to shop during set-up on Friday. General Admission, $3 each day Saturday and Sunday.

TO GET THERE: The show is located in Fisherville, Virginia, close to Lynchburg. Take Interstate 64 to Exit 91.

FOR MORE INFORMATION: Heritage Promotions, P.O. Box 3504, Lynchburg, VA 24503, or telephone 1-804-846-7452.

WEST VIRGINIA

A Penny Saved Antique Mall

This Weston mall is considered a dealer stop by local antiques shop owners, although West Virginia is not the antiques mecca that its sister state is. Sixty dealers, open seven days. Offers a variety of merchandise including rural primitive furniture pieces.

TO GET THERE: Take Interstate 79 to Highway 33.
FOR MORE INFORMATION: Write to 230 Main Street, Weston, WV 26452 or telephone 1-304-269-3258.

WASHINGTON, DC

The Flea Market at Eastern Market

Antiques and collectibles in the Washington, DC area tend to be much more international in origin than those in other states because so many countries have representatives living here.

This market, in the Capitol Hill area, is one of the most historic trade centers in the United States. It started in the early 1800's as a farmers' market, and the market center itself was built in 1873. Today, about 150 dealers generally gather indoors and outdoors on Sundays from March through November, with the exception of the first Sunday in May. Most

ANTIQUES ACROSS AMERICA

of them at this highly rated market are selling antiques and collectibles.

TO GET THERE: The market is one block from Pennsylvania Avenue on Capitol Hill, along Seventh
Street, S.E. The Metro Red Line (subway) has a stop
at Eastern Market, too.
FOR MORE INFORMATION: Write to Tom Rall, 11101 N.
Kentucky St., Arlington, VA 22205, or telephone 1-
703-534-7612.

Georgetown Flea Market

This popular outdoor market, operating in the
heart of one of Washington's most fashionable areas,
also has an eclectic international array of antiques
and collectibles for sale every Sunday beginning with
the first Sunday in March and ending on the last
Sunday before Christmas. No other kinds of merchandise are allowed. More than 130 dealers set up
here, starting at 6 A.M. although sale hours officially
don't start until 9 A.M. This market also delivers.

TO GET THERE: The market is located in a school
parking lot on Wisconsin Avenue, between S and T
Streets N.W., directly across the street from the
Georgetown Safeway supermarket.
FOR MORE INFORMATION: Contact Michael Sussman,
2109 M St., N.W., Washington, DC 20037 or telephone 1-202-296-4989.

CHAPTER SEVEN

ANTIQUES ON THE INTERNET

Beautiful old treasures don't seem to fit naturally into the brave new world spectrum of cyberspace. But believe it or not, the antiques market has already begun to move into the fast lanes of the information superhighway, and it seems clear that the way dealers sell and customers buy is changing right now, and may change even more dramatically in the future.

Dealers, of course, have been using computer programs for a long time. They make it easy to keep track of stock and pay sales taxes, etc. Interaction between dealers and customers didn't begin until a few years ago, when the Internet suddenly became front page news and the computer-literate antique lover started to explore the world of cyber antiques.

The explosive growth experienced in other parts

of the Internet occur here, too. Two months ago, I looked for search references to antiques through a search engine program called Alta Vista and found eleven thousand. Those references were everything from antiques chat rooms to actual antiques shops to books and magazines about antiques in as-published or digest form, ads for related hardware, and other products. That was just a few months ago; today, the number of references in that same search program is 44,000.

I asked a computer-savvy friend of mine, Larkin Anderson, who loves to prowl through antiques malls and flea markets, but doesn't have a lot of knowledge about the subject of antiques and considers herself strictly an amateur enthusiast, to check out Internet listings to see what she might find that she would consider useful.

Her favorites? There are thousands of museum and gallery sites on the World Wide Web. You can wander through collections, picking your choice of subject, and see accurate color videos or still photographs. For the World Wide Web virtual museum pages go to http://www.comlab.ox.ac.uk/archive/othermuseums.html.

You can tap into any library in the world, and call up all kinds of old and new reference books about antiques, from scholarly tomes to current price guides.

In fact, this readily available information makes some dealers a little nervous. Now, if somebody, in an effort to get you to buy a particular piece, spins a tall tale about its origins and value, it's fairly easy to double-check almost instantly via the Internet. This immediate access also has virtually ended regional scams that used to flourish because sellers of deliberately faked merchandise could always move on to another unsuspecting town if they were exposed as fraudulent in the previous one.

The chat rooms about antiques on the Internet are filled with antiques enthusiasts warning each other about all manner of deception and deceit. Recently there was, for instance, a lot of conversation about a weathervane scam that's been going on in the Northeast. Anyone who tapped into this particular chat room could find out who's doing it, how much the phony weathervanes are selling for, and where they've begun to appear on the market.

Internet antiques chat rooms are always filled with people who are helping each other find a particularly arcane replacement part, and telling each other about great auctions and shows. (CompuServe has an extremely interesting chat room, according to Winston Harness, an artisan who handcrafts replacement hardware elements. Harness lives in a tiny town in Missouri, but has access to the entire country, and its residents to him, via http://ourworld .com/HomePages/BRNZCASTER.)

This is the kind of pure information that the Internet was established to provide, and what it does best.

Commerce is another story, although there's no question that using cybermalls and shops is going to be an important part of the antiques trade in the future.

Advertising on the Internet is undergoing such rapid change that it's impossible to predict the eventual shape of this medium right now. A lot of dealers have experimented with ads via the commercial on-line services, in cybermalls or through bulletin boards. They were talked into buying commercial Internet advertising space by some slick-talking snake oil peddlers who promised that putting treasures from the old world on the brave new world's landscape would automatically net any dealer hundreds of new customers every day. Advertising rates were all over the map—$10, $100, $50,000 for a Website shop; it was truly chaotic. People were charging thousands of dollars to create and open Web sites for dealers, when anyone can do it with the help of a $50 computer program. And the ads themselves were usually primitive—a few typed lines of description along with a stock number and a price.

A lot of dealers gave up in disgust because they didn't get the promised increases in business. Many believed, and still do, that it was impossible to sell antiques in cyberspace because customers couldn't actually see and touch the merchandise.

The advent of faster and more powerful computers and printers capable of printing out photos in full color in a matter of a few minutes has made advertising specific merchandise on the Internet a lot easier. Now people can at least see what they're thinking about buying.

Still, according to Mary Schmidt, a dealer in western collectibles who does almost all her business via computer, most of the sales that occur in response to advertising are dealer-to-dealer sales. The average antiques lover isn't routinely prowling through cyberspace the way he or she might hunt through a mall or flea market.

Mary and her mother Barbara operate out of Jackson Hole, Wyoming and specialize in high-end, top quality western cowboy and Indian items like spurs, beadwork, baskets, and jewelry, among others. In addition to selling to other dealers, they also attract the passionate collectors who are focused on one specific object or group. Through their Web site (www.cowboyup.com/Digital Trails) they also provide browsers with show and auction information, monthly feature articles that relate to this area of interest, and comments on useful museum exhibits.

This is the kind of antiques-in-cyberspace operation that works, because it provides useful information along with merchandise available for sale. A lot of the major corporations in this country have found that institutional advertising is, for right now, the best way to utilize the Internet.

Most of the major auction houses now have Web sites, and use them for institutional advertising after a few experiments in conducting auctions by computer proved to be disastrous. Kathleen Guzman, a Christie's vice-president, tried an on-line auction for a charity and says it took her an hour and a half to sell eight lots of lithographs. Christie's auctioneers usually sell at the rate of eighty to one hundred lots an hour.

So Christie's, which gets about twenty thousand visitors to its Web site every month, uses the site to distribute information about upcoming sales by location and category, about how to get an appraisal for an item you'd like to auction, along with tips on how to bid at auctions and the results and prices of past sales. Christie's also sells catalogs to upcoming shows (http://www.christies.com.).

Sotheby's also has a Web site (http://www.sothebys .com) that provides previews of upcoming sales, a worldwide calendar of events, some excerpts from the company's newsletter and descriptions of company-sponsored study programs.

Buying via computer has its own set of problems, and it doesn't much matter whether you're after beaded moccasins or ballpoint pens. Every retailer on the Internet has been struggling with the issue of security. How do you take an order from a customer, and get the required credit card information, without opening up vast opportunities for fraud?

If you're going to buy antiques through an on-line dealer, first make sure before you pay that you have some kind of thorough guarantee. The dealer should be able to fax you a copy of your written guarantee agreement. You'll want the dealer to promise a full refund if the advertised merchandise is not what he or she says it is. When you commit to purchase, the dealer also ought to supply a detailed assessment of its condition, a statement that lists any tiny imperfections or wear. Actually this protects both the customer and the dealer. Also make sure you have a commitment to a delivery date. You won't get the dealer to promise you'll have the chair next Tuesday, but you can ask for a written assurance that your purchase will be shipped within the next two weeks or month, for example.

Then, when you have all the details spelled out, including any additional shipping charges, go to a telephone and make your payment arrangements confidentially.

When she was exploring the world of cyber antiques, Larkin discovered to her delight that she could shop just as easily for antiques in Holland via her computer as she could anywhere in the United States. Her only problem was she couldn't figure out the photo captions or the exchange rate for Dutch currency. But she was able to call up dozens of photos of antique European sofas and chairs available through a dealer in Holland, and she also could have, had she decided to buy, used the services of an international shopping facilitator who would have, for a fee, converted the currency, translated the captions, and arranged shipping and payment.

Ed Burke, who is a writer and dealer, does a column for one of my favorite trade papers, *MassBay Antiques*. He thinks international trade in antiques is the true future of the market, and also the arena in which sellers are going to be able to make the most profit.

He says, "The Internet is going to do to the worldwide antiques market what trade papers, shows, and group shops did for the American antiques marketplace, de-regionalizing the selling price.

"Many American antiques and collectibles items sell for ten to twenty times the standard U.S. price in Japan, Sweden, Italy, Germany, England, and Canada.

"Ten years ago, Canadian cupboards were worth more in America than in Canada. Today the price for a quality Canadian cupboard is three to five times greater in Canada. Canadian dealers are now coming to the States to buy back the cupboards they sold just ten years ago. If you are an antiques dealer and have in stock Canadian cupboards, advertising these cupboards on the Internet will bring your shop Canadian buyers.

"Cowboy and western collectibles are worth their weight in gold in Japan and in Germany. An inexpensive ad on the Internet can open these markets to a rural New England dealer. A Charles Eames chair sells for $350 in Sweden. The same chair sells for $35 in Brimfield.

"The winners in antique cyberspace will be the dealers who figure out how to get the thirty-five dollar Brimfield chair to Sweden and the cowboy and western collectibles to Japan and Germany."

Another important note to keep in mind: The cyber antiques world is a very promising place right now for entrepreneurs who are interested in establishing computer-based businesses. Already, computer-driven search agencies to help you find the antiques or collectibles you need are proliferating, as are businesses that will provide you with specialized price guides, or any other kind of related information you may need.

Internet Antique Connections

Real Time Antiques Market on the web at http://www.rtam.com. Buyers sign up for categories that interest them and are instantly notified via e-mail of items for sale in their chosen areas of interest as soon as a seller posts them on the Internet. Sellers pay no fee; the "show" also offers a free link to photos or the seller's web page. Sign-up fee for buyers, $9.95 per year. Mail address: P.O. Box 383a, Manchester, NH 03105-0383.

Antique Networking: On-line database for dealers and collectors. Search engine. Startup, $150 enrollment plus a fee of $24.95 per month for unlimited ads to sell. Search packets of fifty searches, $25. Unlimited searches, $50 per month. (http://www.antiqnet.com.) or telephone 1-800-400-8674.

ArtNet Auctions on-line: Fine arts database. Custom searches. Cost, $1.75 per minute. (http://www.artnet.com) or telephone 1-800-427-8638.

Antique & Collectible Exchange: An on-line marketplace for people who want to advertise items for sale with color photos. $195 per year. (http://www.tace.com) or telephone 1-800-643-2204.

Collector On-Line Web site for ads, auction calendar, and club directories. Ad costs vary. (http://collectoronline .com/collect) or telephone 1-800-546-2941.

Collector's SuperMall: Antique Trader publications' database of shows and auctions, directories, book list. Searches are free. Ads cost $5 and up. (http://www.csmonline .com) or telephone 1-800-364-5593.

Intellasearch: On-line marketplace and price guide for eighteen hundred collectibles categories. $12.95 per month after software purchase of $25 to $45 in programs. (http://www.intellasearch.com) or telephone 1-800-947-5390.

CHAPTER EIGHT

SOUTHERN REGION

Kentucky, Tennessee, Georgia, Alabama,
Louisiana, Mississippi, Florida

The 450-Mile Long Yard Sale

Yes, it's true. This yard sale starts in Covington, Kentucky, right across the Ohio River from Cincinnati, Ohio, and winds its way south down the Route 127 corridor, also known as the Dixie Highway, for 450 miles of truly delicious antiquing.

Route 127 extends from Interstate 71/75 in Covington, where you pick it up, then south through Kentucky and across Tennessee to Chattanooga, where the Lookout Mountain Parkway continues. It passes through one corner of Georgia and ends in Gadsden, Alabama.

There's absolutely everything along the road, from small sales in front yards where local residents display antiques and collectibles they've been saving to sell for a year, to professionally organized flea markets or shows sponsored by churches, charities, or dealers themselves. At the last sale, for example, there was a large flea market organized by the Swallow Field Central Baptist Church to help raise funds for a parishioner's bone marrow transplant, and in Cumberland Gap, Tennessee, the Cumberland Gap General Store, an antiques mall with 150 dealers, hosted its usual outdoor show.

Had you driven down this road last year—the sale is always conducted in the middle of August—you would have found some incredibly beautiful antique furniture such as a cherry five-drawer bureau that was a few hundred dollars but would sell for several thousand in a city, some ancient headstones from a graveyard that apparently disappeared in the course of a development, to local produce or canned goods—cherries, homemade pies, candy, etc.—bicycles, handmade baskets old and new, folk art, glassware, pottery, Adirondack chairs and tables, and just about everything else, including puppies and kittens.

There are thousands of vendors along the way. State officials say that one hundred thousand people participate in this sale, and of course, thousands more arrive to buy.

Expect a few bare stretches of highway; most of the sales, even those by single families or individuals, seem to be grouped in clusters. So you may drive a few miles and see nothing, then suddenly come upon a dozen sales all set up along one small section of the road.

The yard sale opens officially on Thursday and continues through Friday, Saturday, and Sunday on the designated weekend. Dealers, of course, try to get started early Thursday morning, but they can't clean out all the great bargains right away because the sale is just too long for one person to see everything in one day. A lot of vendors don't even bother setting out their wares until Saturday, because most customers won't start to drive the route until then.

This sale attracts people from as far away as Alaska and California who fly in just to make the drive. The best airport destinations are Nashville, Tennessee, Lexington, Kentucky, or Louisville, Kentucky in addition to Cincinnati.

Experienced hunters along this route seem to like to start a little south of Covington, perhaps in Frankfort, Tennessee, and divide the search into two segments, one concentrating on the northern half of the Route, in Kentucky and northern Tennessee; then traveling on the second day all the way south into Georgia and Alabama.

This yard sale began ten years ago when a county executive in Fentress County, Tennessee realized that Route 127 was losing a lot of business because travelers were ignoring it in favor of the Interstate. It has expanded every year since then, and is now administered by chambers of commerce in four states.

FOR MORE INFORMATION: Write the Fentress County Chamber of Commerce, P.O. Box 1294, Jamestown, Tennessee, 38556 for information about the sale and other tourist attractions along the way, plus travel information and a map. Or telephone the Highway 127 sale hotline at 1-800-327-3945.

KENTUCKY

Louisville

The Kentucky State Fairgrounds and Expo Center are the location for Kentucky's largest almost monthly antiques market. Although the dates vary, it is usually at the beginning of the month and is an extremely well-attended event that often attracts two thousand dealers. Open Friday, Saturday, and Sunday, also on Mondays during holiday weekends.

TO GET THERE: Interstate 65 north or south to Interstate 264, east to Exit 11.

FOR MORE INFORMATION: Telephone 1-502-456-2244 or write to Stewart Promotions, 2950 Breckinridge Lane, Ste 4A, Louisville, KY 40220.

Lexington, Kentucky Summer Antique & Collectibles Show

This show, with an average 150 dealers, takes place once a month for three days from April through October. It's located in the Lexington Loose Leaf Tobacco Warehouse, which in November reverts to its real purpose—the sale of tobacco.

During its antiques phase, though, no other products except for collectibles are allowed and there is always a wide variety of antiques, including rural primitive furniture and folk art. Free admission and parking.

TO GET THERE: Interstate 75 to Exit 113, south to Angliana Avenue.

FOR MORE INFORMATION: Telephone 1-606-255-7309

TENNESSEE

Esau's Antique & Collectible Market

Located in the foothills of the Smokey Mountains, this market has been a focal point for southern dealers to come to buy for 21 years. More than 350 dealers from at least nine surrounding states usually set up here on the third weekend of every month, Saturdays and Sundays, 9 to 5.

Owner Ralph Greene keeps his show pleasant and

tasteful and doesn't allow anything other than antiques and collectibles to be sold by his vendors. "No tube socks," he says.

Three times a year, the market does "extravaganzas," special heavily promoted three-day antiques weekends that drawn another 500 dealers. They are always conducted in April, July and October.

The monthly markets are $3 admission good for both days; the extravaganzas are $5 for both days, with an early buyers' admission of $6 for Fridays.

TO GET THERE: The market is located at the Fairgrounds in Chilohowee Park. Take Interstate 40 to Exit 392, Rutledge Pike.

FOR MORE INFORMATION: Write to ESAU, Inc., P.O. Box 50096, Knoxville, TN 37950, or telephone 1-800-588-ESAU.

GEORGIA

Scott Antique Markets

This is a long-established antiques and collectibles market that now has two adjacent locations at the Atlanta Exposition Center in Atlanta, Georgia. Open monthly from November through July, it is always held on the second weekend of the month.

There are 1,250 exhibitor booths available each month.

TO GET THERE: Both the north and south fields are located three miles east of the Atlanta Airport on Interstate 285 at Exit 40, Jonesboro Rd.

FOR MORE INFORMATION: Write Scott Antique Markets, P.O. Box 60, Bremen, OH, 43107. Telephone 1-614-569-4112.

ADDENDUM: Atlanta has two other extremely popular flea markets that attract antiquers. There's one at the Lakewood Fairgrounds, also on the second weekend of the month, telephone 1-404-622-4488; and on the fourth weekend of the month, the Pride of Dixie market is held at the North Atlanta Trade Center, telephone 1-614-998-6900.

Folkfest

Folk art, particularly antique folk art, is generating a lot of collecting enthusiasm now, with articles in trade newspapers and magazines focusing regularly on this subject. To get a good grounding in folk art, check out the eighty dealers who gather on the third weekend in August every year at the North Atlanta Trade Center (where the Pride of Dixie Antique Shows take place) to display the best in folk art, with some special emphasis on older works by anonymous artists, especially African-Americans.

There is a $15 fee for opening night, which also includes a cocktail party and show program, on Friday. Regular admission, $5 good for both Saturday and Sunday.

In the spring, usually in March, show organizers Steve and Amy Slotin also produce a folk art auction which draws dealers from virtually everywhere.

TO GET THERE: Interstate 85 in Atlanta to Indian Trail, exit 38,m east on Indian Trail, right on Oakbrook Parkway, right on Jeurgens Court.

FOR MORE INFORMATION: To get an advance notice of the auction or show, write to Steve and Amy Slotin at 5967 Blackberry Lane, Buford, GA 30518, or telephone 1-770-932-1000.

ALABAMA

Olde Mill Antique Mall & Village

This hundred-year-old former cotton mill has sixty-eight thousand square feet of antiques and collectibles offered by two hundred dealers. There's everything from fine antique furniture to baseball cards and other collectibles. Outside, an additional ten stores make up the Olde Mill Village, operated by individual dealers. On weekends, the Olde Mill also sponsors a flea market.

TO GET THERE: The Olde Mill is located in Oxford, Alabama, an hour from Birmingham, ninety minutes from Atlanta. Interstate 20 to Exit 185.

FOR MORE INFORMATION: Write to P.O. Box 3118, Oxford, AL, 36203. Telephone 1-205-835-0599.

ADDENDUM: While you're in the area, check out the small, picturesque town of Anniston, Alabama. The downtown area is filled with attractive antiques shops.

LOUISIANA

Fireside Antiques

This is one of the premier antiques shops in this country, specializing in fine European antiques from nine countries. It is the largest importer of French furniture in the country, according to owner Cheri McDaniel who has six employees in France and two in England working full time to find shipments for her 16,000 sq. ft. store.

She says half her customers come from out of state, from all parts of the country. She has shipped antiques to every part of the country, including Alaska.

Open seven days. High tea is served Tuesday through Saturday.

TO GET THERE: Fireside is located in Baton Rouge, Louisiana, which is just a few miles northwest of New Orleans. Take Interstate 10 from east or west.

FOR MORE INFORMATION: Write Cheri McDaniel, Fireside Antiques, 14007 Perkins Rd, Baton Rouge, LA 70810.

Magazine Street, New Orleans

There are at least 300 antiques dealers operating along New Orleans' Magazine Street, the city's most popular antique row. There are also a number of antiques shops in the French Quarter, most of them established for a long time.

ADDENDUM: While you're in Louisiana, it's worth the trip—about 35 miles, north of New Orleans on Interstate 55—to Ponchatoula, a small town with a large concentration of antiques dealers.

MISSISSIPPI

Old Friends Arts, Crafts and Antique Show

Ten times a year, this weekend market takes place in the Trade Mart Building at the State Fairgrounds in Jackson. It serves as a regular showplace for more than 125 antiques dealers and artists or artisans, and has a loyal following. Lots of glassware, and of course folk art.

TO GET THERE: Interstates 20 and 55 intersect in the center of Jackson. The Fairgrounds exit is marked.

FOR MORE INFORMATION: Write to show organizer Bettie Emery, P.O. Box 397, Terry, MS 39170 or telephone 1-601-878-6600.

Washington Street Antiques

The historic Civil War town of Vicksburg is not only beautiful, with its many restored antebellum mansions, but replete with antiques shops large and small.

Washington Street Antiques is one of the largest and most elaborate. It is housed in an historic three-story building that was the town's fashion center years ago, and comes complete with lavish fixtures, including crystal chandeliers. The building is large—25,000 sq. ft.—and has 25 dealers currently. There are at least 100 other dealers in Vicksburg in various malls and shops.

TO GET THERE: Take Highway 220 from Jackson and get off at Exit 4B, also called Clay Street.

FOR MORE INFORMATION: Write to mall owner Allison Pittman at 1305 Washington Street, Vicksburg, MS 39180, or telephone 1-601-636-3700.

Natchez

A delightful southern town, Natchez has one of the largest concentrations of dealers in the state.

There are dozens of shops in town, including the Hal Garner Antiques shops—three restored buildings that house a collection of fine English-style antiques, an interior design service and a gift shop.

There are also five small malls, including the Commercial Bank, another historic building.

TO GET THERE: Natchez is at the western edge of the state, close to the Louisiana border. Take Interstate 84 west.

FOR MORE INFORMATION: The Commercial Bank, 1-601-442-8400; or Hal Garner Antiques, 1-601-445-8416.

FLORIDA

Renningers

The famous Renningers in Pennsylvania has expanded to Florida, and here, on 115 acres with forty-thousand square feet of selling space, is the state's largest gathering of dealers. It is open every weekend on Saturday and Sunday, year-round.

It has attracted a lot of dealers from the Northeast who got tired of lugging merchandise through ice and snow and decided to retire to Florida. Once here, of course, they couldn't stay away from antiques and now spend their weekends selling in Mount Dora, Florida. There are outdoor spaces and air-conditioned indoor booths. Admission is free.

The Florida branch also does three annual "extravaganza" weekends, held in November, January, and February, when travel to the southern states is at its peak. You do have to pay admission to get into these shows.

Dealers are strictly warned not to bring reproduction merchandise here, but expect a little of everything. There are a lot of folk art dealers. If you want to stay overnight, campgrounds, RV parks, and motels abound.

TO GET THERE: Mount Dora isn't too far from Disney World; it's just twenty miles north of Orlando on Route 441.

FOR MORE INFORMATION: Write to P.O. Box 1699, Mt. Dora, FL, 32757-1699. Telephone 1-352-383-8393, Thursday—Sunday.

Webster Farmer's Market

This is where you get to ride on Big Al, a twelve-foot-long real alligator (now stuffed) who hangs out at Carol Bornemann's antiques market, which is part of the Webster complex.

This market started in the Depression years because local farmers were too poor to get their crops to market, so they banded together to attract customers who would come to them. Immediately successful, it's been running now since 1937 and is one of the oldest operating flea markets in the United States. In Florida, it's regarded as one of the state's top ten tourist attractions.

The town of Webster is tiny: only one thousand people live here. But on market day the population swells to forty thousand. The market is unique because it's open only on Mondays.

As a result, dealers who have other shops can come here to sell on a day that's normally slow in the antiques business. In the summer months, Webster may host only three hundred to four hundred dealers, but in the winter months, as it gets colder up north, that figure may jump to as many as three thousand dealers all showing at one time. The best times to go, however, are the three-day holiday weekends, because that's when the most dealers arrive.

Although the Webster Farmer's Market is the oldest and largest here, three other markets operate in adjacent fields. There's Carol Bornemann's Wee Flea Market, Webster West Side, and a fourth, with no official name, run by Martha Sparkman.

You don't have to pay admission to get into any of the markets. Parking is $2 to $4 depending upon vehicle size.

TO GET THERE: Webster is one hour north of Tampa and one hour west of Orlando, four miles north of Highway 50 on Highway 471, also called Market Boulevard.

FOR MORE INFORMATION: Telephone 1-352-793-2021

CHAPTER NINE

IS IT A FAKE?

Let me tell you about an auction that I went to in a little northern Colorado town. All the local dealers and collectors were excited because this was a big-time auction house from Denver, clearing out a few estates and bringing all these super goodies up to us in the hinterlands.

The first thing I saw when I walked in to check out the lots that were going to be offered for sale was a fabulous doll carriage. It was really terrific, Victorian, with wicker curlicues decorating the frame, and it certainly seemed old. Wooden wheels, aged and cracked black oilcloth basket and bonnet, even the right amount of fading and wear inside for a piece at least one hundred years old.

I loved it and I would have bid on it, too, if I hadn't looked up to see a row of twenty other doll

carriages exactly like it on top of a set of cupboards also waiting to be sold.

The auctioneer was very careful; he never actually said these doll buggies were antiques; he just talked about the old-fashioned wicker trim, and the fact that buggies like this usually sold for fifteen hundred dollars in the big antiques stores. That made the $150 he was asking for look good, and he sold a lot of these carriages that day. They didn't go to dealers, who realized what was going on, but to doll enthusiasts who hadn't caught on and thought they were picking up huge bargains.

This auction was really useful because it turned into a cram course on fake antiques. It looked as though someone had made a fast pass through a lot of antiques shops, figured what was most desirable, and then copied all of it.

There were painted wooden chests, Pennsylvania Dutch cradles, washstand pitchers and bowls, those cute little ice cream parlor wire chairs and tables—both child and doll size—Remington and Russell western bronzes, tables, chairs, sleigh bells, dolls.

The auction house was not the least bit apologetic about selling any of it. When one woman who bought a doll went up to one of the auctioneer's assistants to complain that the doll was a fake, the man said, and I heard him: "It's not fake! It's authentic. It's a genuine authentic reproduction!"

And the cut glass! Unless I can pick it up for eight bucks at a yard sale, I won't even touch a piece of

cut glass. Nor would I buy it without a written statement of authenticity from the seller, and preferably
a provenance as well.

The copies that were sold at this auction were
beautiful and abundant, almost impossible to tell
from the genuine old cut glass.

One vase I especially admired was so carefully
faked it included a tiny chip at the top for authenticity and even an etched signature on the bottom. It
was selling for about $150, which would have been
a huge bargain for the real thing, but was not so
cheap for a copy.

This "repro" cut glass is around everywhere, from
the eastern end of Long Island to the Pacific Coast.
The going rate for a medium-sized bowl ought to be
$50 to $75, which is what Bloomingdale's in New
York sells it for new. Unfortunately, it's all over antiques shops for $200 and up. Watch out for it.

(You did know, didn't you, that the best way to
check for chips in glassware is by running your finger over the rims, base, and all edges. You will be
able to feel any little chips or chinks a lot more
quickly than you can see them.)

Deliberate fakes, like the cut glass, are flooding
the country. These are not the obvious reproductions you often find in import stores which occasionally make their way into the more eclectic antiques
malls simply because some dealers are fairly new to
the game and not skilled enough yet to be able to
tell the difference. Everyone's seen them—the old

cobalt blue Mr. Peanut cookie jar, the pink Depression glass patterns, the chocolate molds, and milk glass chicken-on-a-nest containers. These are, instead, meticulously crafted to look genuine and are so well done they can fool even the experts.

In the past couple of weeks, I've seen two wicker doll sleighs with somewhat elaborate iron runners in two different antiques shops, priced at $225 and $275 respectively. I own one of these sleighs myself and use it as part of my Christmas decorating. I bought it new at a discount store in the middle of Nebraska a couple of years ago and I paid $39 for it.

A lot of these new, practically impeccable reproductions seem to be coming to the United States from the Philippines and a few points further east—Thailand, Malaysia, Indonesia, Taiwan and China—where labor is still cheap and import laws are favorable.

Some of these products actually are a better buy than the authentic antique versions, especially if they are going to be put to daily use. A Chinese handmade patchwork quilt, for example, is a much better choice for a child's bedroom than the real thing. Chinese quilts have in fact had a great impact on the quilt market within the antiques world. For a long time, quilt prices did nothing but go up. Now they are not only stable, but actually dropping unless the quilt has extraordinary quality.

Battenberg lace and crocheted tablecloths, runners, and bedspreads are now available so inexpensively that they, too, have affected the market for these products. They're also a decorator's dream come true. No more trying to stretch a scant double into a spread for a queen-size bed. And some of the more amusing Victorian reproductions—those carved wooden standing bears that support a bench, rocking horses, or doll houses—make great room accents, especially when you have growing children and know that your "antiques" are going to be subject to a lot of wear and tear. Real antique rocking horses, by the way, usually don't have much in the way of a mane or a tail. Repros always seem to have luxuriant ones.

Buying reproductions isn't a problem as long as they're sold as such and priced accordingly. But when you pay a stiff price for something that turns out to be worth about ten percent of what it just cost you, you have a right to be outraged.

This issue never used to affect the ordinary collector, who was usually just interested in antiques at the lower end of the market, because there wasn't enough money in butter churns, to use an example, to make their duplication worthwhile. That's no longer true. The combination of readily available, inexpensive labor and strong consumer demand makes everything fair game, from cast-iron banks to early pine furniture. They age the banks in the Far East by burying them for a month or two. The early pine gets that way because it's been hit with chains to dent and age it.

Here's how it all begins. Collectors are charmed by an attractive and inexpensive object, and begin to buy it up. Sooner or later, it starts to appear in decorating magazines, by which time it's hot. Everybody wants one and there aren't enough around to meet the demand. Suddenly, the reproductions start to appear.

Consider the simple salt-and-pepper shaker sets. They were popular souvenirs in the nineteen-twenties, thirties, and forties when Americans first began to tour their country by car and liked to buy small keepsakes that didn't take up much room. Almost every middle-class kitchen had a wall full of them until they began to fade in popularity in the late fifties and sixties. Even ten years ago, there were very few people who would admit to becoming entranced by salt-and-pepper shakers. Auctioneers who had to dispose of them during one of those all-purpose estate sales would sell them by the box full.

Now, salt-and-pepper shakers have become fashionable again and have become the center of attention for an entire subculture of new collectors. There are books, price guides, conventions, newsletters and clubs, and some of the early, hard-to-find pairs, such as the International Sweethearts, little boy and girl couples wearing various national costumes, are worth hundreds of dollars. Is it surprising that manufacturers begin to dig out some old molds, or create new molds that look old, to cash in on a lucrative new market? Of course not.

I watched this kind of trend take off in my own little shop with kerosene lanterns. Molded clear glass nineteenth-century or early twentieth-century kerosene lanterns in reasonable condition used to sell for $25 to $30 each, with very elaborate molded or pressed glass models, especially Aladdins, bringing a higher price of about $150. Then Mary Emmerling, who writes all those wonderfully stylish country decorating books, had her own Sag Harbor summer house photographed for a magazine spread. In one of the photos, a half-dozen clear glass lanterns in different sizes and shapes were clustered at one end of a primitive harvest table.

That's all it took. From the day that issue of *Country Living* hit the stands, and for months afterward, I couldn't keep clear glass lanterns in my store. I'd buy them, put them out, and they'd be sold in a day or two. They began to increase in price in my dealer sources next, so that even the colored glass base lanterns that are relatively modern began to get more expensive. The six- or eight-sided Eagle lantern with the colored base used to show up routinely at yard sales for about three dollars; you could buy them at flea markets for ten. Now, they are $20 and $25 everywhere and it's all Mary's fault. Incidentally, if you can still find a Eagle inexpensively at a yard sale, snap it up, because heavy-duty kerosene lamp collectors say prices are going to go up.

There are some interesting home-grown fakes out there, too. Not everything is manufactured overseas.

A lot of shops are beginning to display a very attractive wooden cart known variously as a goat cart, a hay cart, a dog cart, or a gypsy cart. It has wooden wheels with metal rims, open slat sides that splay out a little bit, and a wooden handle.

It usually sells for around $500, so I was really excited when I found a whole group of them being sold at an auction in the Midwest. They were selling for $200 to $300 and I was sure that when the auctioneer reached the last few, they'd drop lower than that. But another dealer from Chicago, who was standing next to me at the sale, warned me that they were just awfully good reproductions and told me they never sold for less than $200 each because the maker had a shill at the auction who made sure the price never got any lower. They are made, I'm told, in Ohio.

Not that Ohio is a hotbed of deceit or anything, but it's also the home of the fake nineteenth-century political quilt. The *Maine Antique Digest* got curious when a lot of these interesting red, white, and blue quilts began to show up on the market and were subsequently identified as fakes traced to a dealer in Ohio. These quilts incorporate patriotic themes and/ or political slogans, and are prime examples of Early American folk art. They sell for several thousand dollars if real, which is why someone decided to start making them again. They are very good; I looked closely at one and never would have guessed it was a copy. The fabric had just the right shadings of wear and age. It was priced at $1,600, a good price if it had been genuine, but not much of a buy for something made a month earlier.

Sometimes it seems there's almost nothing now that someone hasn't tried to fake. For a while, every dealer I knew got caught by an ingenious fellow who took old buttons, glued them to long, sharpened pieces of wire and sold them as antique hatpins. Everybody bought them, and I would have, too, because they're extremely attractive, but he disappeared before I had a chance.

How do you protect yourself against rip-offs? I try to stick to a fairly simple equation: the price you pay for anything ought to be in direct proportion to its provenance.

Provenance is, of course, the history of the piece. When one of the top dealers sells a bureau or desk for a five or six-figure price, provenance means solid, written proof that the piece is indeed a seventeenth- or eighteenth-century furniture masterpiece. Most of us needn't be so fussy. You're not asking a dealer to sign a statement in blood. But if you're investing in a big-ticket purchase like a bureau, it's reasonable to expect it to be what the dealer told you it was and to have that information in writing.

I would expect the dealer to accompany the sale with some kind of guarantee, even if it's just a scribbled description on the sales slip that says "late nineteenth-century spoon-carved three-drawer bureau, maple."

Most antiques shops have "no return" or "return for credit only" policies, but I think it's fair to insist that the dealer add to his guarantee that you will be able to get your money back if the item turns out to be a reproduction or outright fake.

The best insurance against being stuck with a fake is your own expert eye. Jonathan Grant, the English neurosurgeon who writes as Jonathan Gash and created Lovejoy, the detective/antique dealer, made his character a "divvy"—a person with such a highly developed sixth sense that he can tell the true antique from the fake intuitively. Grant says that everyone has the ability to hear that little internal chime of recognition in one area of life or another. You can make it ding yourself in response to genuine antiques by looking and looking and looking and learning while you look.

Because no one has the time to become an expert on everything, pick the collectibles or antiques you find most interesting and focus your attention there. Read as many books and price guides as you can and never miss a chance to wander through an antiques shop or a museum. Some of the small, eccentric museums that dot the United States are terrific—the best possible research bargain you can get because you're able to learn so much in a couple of hours. And in these smaller museums, docents tend to be much more willing to spend time telling you what they know about the collection. Often their range of knowledge is extraordinary.

My personal favorite is the museum pioneer village in Encampment, Wyoming, a little town of no more than six hundred people near Interstate 80 between Rawlins and Laramie. Authentic buildings were moved to the site to create a frontier town, and the local residents must never have given anything away because they furnished the entire restoration out of their own barns and attics, donating everything from fabulous Victorian ball gowns to giant bear traps.

The village has a lot of unusual elements, including a two story outhouse (it snows a lot in Wyoming), a livery stable with a horse-drawn fire engine, and even a carpenter's shop where I saw for the first time a truly grisly but fascinating object—a wicker coffin to hold a body and at the same time provide some necessary ventilation until the carpenter could build a casket for burial. I've only seen one other, and it's in an antiques mall in New York City. The dealer who owns it doesn't know what it is and I wouldn't have either if I hadn't gone to Encampment.

It's never a waste of time to check out import stores like Pier One, the Bombay Company, or the Pottery Barn, and you should order all the catalogs you can from places like Trifles or Yield House. All these interior design chains sell wonderfully designed new "antiques," and it helps to familiarize yourself with their merchandise, which sometimes turns up as authentic in malls and flea markets.

The more you look, the more you read, the more

you'll be educating your eye and developing that sixth sense so you can quickly see, for example, that Depression glass reproductions are almost always a lot heavier and a little more crudely made than the real ones, while the exact opposite is true for wicker. Old wicker is always heavier and may seem to be a little more clumsy than the new, lightweight imports.

It was not unusual, for example, to find china marked "Limoges" even in fairly modest homes, and it shows up regularly all over the country. There are, however, different kinds of Limoges, because Limoges is a place, not a brand name, and dozens of manufacturers used it on their china. Haviland is a prized china label to look for, with or without the word Limoges, as are Copeland, Spode, and Wedgewood, among others. Sometimes, you'll just see a country of origin—Bavaria, Hungary, Ireland— or a manufacturer's mark. These marks can be a trial because learning to recognize them could take a lifetime, but if you familiarize yourself with some of the major company's marks, you will be well ahead of most of the other people hunting for treasures.

In the late nineteenth and early twentieth century, art glass was extremely popular in both the United States and Europe. Tiffany is probably the most recognizable name in art glass. But Tiffany, like a lot of other manufacturers of art glass, did not always mark pieces but used paper labels instead.

Don't automatically pass over a beautiful piece of glass just because it doesn't have a name engraved in the bottom. It may be worth a small fortune if it's Loetz, Tiffany, Galle or any of the other art nouveau glassmakers.

Less expensive, but still extremely collectible, are the colored glass bowls, vases, pitchers, etc., made by firms like Heisey, Fostoria, or Cambridge. And then, of course, there is Depression glass, available in dozens of patterns and colors. Some of the more rare Depression glass patterns can bring hundreds of dollars for a single piece; others sell for only a few dollars each, so a Depression glass price guide— make sure it's illustrated—is a good idea if you find this glass appealing.

Art pottery is another huge collecting category. Devotees of Roseville, Hull, Weller, or the less expensive McCoy, have driven the price for these pieces up and up.

Costume jewelry practically forms its own subculture in the antiques world. One of the reasons so many dealers like to specialize in jewelry is that it's easy to transport; there's no heavy lifting involved. This is also a category in collecting in which age doesn't seem to matter too much. Because so many people deal in jewelry, it's progressively harder to find the huge bargains you used to be able to grab at yard sales a few years ago. However, look for names like Kenneth Jay Lane whose seventies designs (and copies) sell for hundreds. Other good jew-

Some Really Clever Fakes

1. Painted Pennsylvania Dutch wooden chests.
The easiest way to identify a fake is by the painting itself.
It may be artfully faded, but the colors are very modern,
very different from the shades in use during the eighteenth and nineteenth century. A lot of artsy detail is
another good clue. And check the interior of the chest. If
it seems too new, watch out.

2. Iron-rimmed wooden wheels. Attached to old
wagons and carriages, also on toy tricycles, carts, baby
carriages, doll strollers, and miniature sulkies. Look
closely at the wheels first. If the wooden wheel frame fits
exactly against the surrounding metal rim, with no signs
of wear at all, chances are good the piece is a fake. On
these wooded iron-rimmed wheels, constant problems developed because the wood shrank and expanded in different weather conditions. As a result, the iron loosened
and often came off. The pioneers complained about this
all the time and there is an entire group of early tools
that were created to deal with the problems of wooden
wheels. There should be signs of wear even on small
toy items.

3. Logo china, especially ironstone. You'll see a lot
now that looks very genuine, with logos from passenger
ships or from first-class hotels. All of this is new, and it's
starting to filter into antiques malls as old. Be very careful
if you're going to invest in a complete set. Check for signs
of wear, which will be apparent at the back of the dinner
plate, for example.

4. Bowls. Because yellow ware, redware, or other pottery bowls have so much appeal in country kitchens,
many have been remade from the original molds. The
yellow ware with the broad blue strip banding is new, as

are the solid blue or those with a molded rim design. Again, look for signs of wear.

5. Copper pots with a silver overlay. These are hand-hammered and are indeed handmade, but they're from Turkey and they're brand new. Almost all the copper you see now in antiques malls seems to be reproduction; genuine early pieces are very rare. Sometimes the repros are even corroded a bit for authenticity.

6. Turquoise jewelry. A lot of the southwestern-style jewelry on the market today is actually from Taiwan or the Philippines, and the turquoise itself is ground stone that's been reformed with the help of plastic. If the stone is smooth and shiny, with no traces of other minerals it's often fake. Good Indian jewelry is always marked and often signed.

7. Ship Models. They look important and impressive and every other antiques shop seems to have one in the window, but ship models—wooden sailing ships, yachts, even steamships—are almost always reproduction now. If you can't live without one, make sure you get a guarantee of authenticity.

8. Weathervanes. They seem to be incredibly easy to fake because they're all over. Copper, aged with acid to get that nice green tint, is particularly prevalent and usually is priced at $150. There are also more primitive models—horses cut from sheet metal with tin snips and then aged with rust, for example—that sell for much more. Ask yourself: If they're very elaborate and in good condition, with no bullet holes, missing bits, etc., how could they have been outdoors? The real ones go for thousands.

elry names to look for: Weiss, Corocraft, Eisenberg, Ciner, Hobe, Boucher and Lisner.

It's still possible to find real gems among the costume jewelry pieces on the market, even when sold by knowledgeable dealers. Garnets were very popular right around the time of the mass emigrations to this country from Europe. The garnets are sometimes overlooked because they were often set in brass, instead of gold. Aquamarines are also interesting. These pale blue stones were the only gems other than diamonds that young women were allowed to wear when they were presented at court in England, and as a result, aquamarines were popular everywhere until the custom of court presentations died out before World War Two. You'll often find them in inexpensive settings.

There are ardent collectors looking for all the small, homey items that people used in their kitchens and laundries up through the forties, including the humble glass milk bottle, canning jars (especially aqua or green), wooden ironing boards, washboards, utensils, egg beaters, rolling pins and glass refrigerator storage containers.

Almost any kind of decorative sign, from old Coca-Cola signs to those winged DeKalb corn signs, are extremely collectible. Even the paper labeled panels from fruitboxes have an enthusiastic following.

CHAPTER TEN

CENTRAL PLAINS REGION

Iowa, Kansas, Missouri, Nebraska, Oklahoma, Arkansas

Iowa

Walnut

Like Mullica Hill in New Jersey, Walnut was a disappearing community until the sale of antiques took over as the town's primary business. Now shops flourish throughout the small town, with more added each year.

Thirty years ago, a local dealer, Bill Johnson, organized a small antiques show in the little town's park. Since then, most of the vacant storefronts on Main Street have been filled with antiques, and today, out of Walnut's total population of nine hundred, 250 dealers are permanent residents here.

Walnut is open year-round, but the number of visitors peaks in June, when the village conducts its annual AmVet charity antiques show and the whole town—well, sixteen blocks, which is almost all of Walnut—turns into an open-air antiques market, with close to fifteen hundred dealers.

To prevent gridlock, busses take visitors from parking lots on the edge of town to the antiques area, and golf carts take your packages back to your car for you. Local organizations also provide food booths and evening meals, because Walnut couldn't possibly feed the usual crowd of thirty thousand visitors in its restaurants.

The town also has initiated a special Christmas show, called the Christmas Walk, to attract Christmas shoppers to the area.

TO GET THERE: Walnut is one mile south of Interstate 80 at Exit 46, 50 miles east of Omaha.
FOR MORE INFORMATION: Write Antique Bill Johnson at P.O. Box 7, Walnut, IA, 51577 or telephone 712-784-3046.

Banowetz Antique Malls

Maquoketa, Iowa, between Davenport and Dubuque at the eastern edge of the state, offers visitors what it likes to call "the ultimate antique experience" in two locations within the perimeters of the small town. One section is at the junction of High-

ways 61 and 64; the other, one mile north on Highway 61.

More than 150 dealers sell from the two malls,
and special event promotions during the year bring
hundreds more to town. The major annual event is
the July 4th weekend show and sale.

TO GET THERE: Maquoketa is a few miles north of
Interstate 80 on Highway 61.

FOR MORE INFORMATION: Write Banowitz Antique
Mall, 122 McKinsey Drive, Maquoketa, Iowa, 52060
or telephone 1-319-652-2359.

McGregor

This small town on the banks of the Mississippi
River has been a trading post for two centuries, ever
since Indian trappers brought their furs to the small
trading post run by a Scottish fur buyer named
McGregor.

At one point in history, McGregor's population
was bigger than Chicago's because the town was a
major commercial center. Now it has about 860 residents, many of whom have renovated some of the
town's strikingly beautiful waterfront homes and
converted them into antiques shops. The largest
group shop in town is the McGregor Antique Mall,
with fifty dealers. Another dozen shops hold from
one to five more dealers each. You can expect to
find a lot of nice country primitives here, as well as

extensive selections of collectible glassware and other small antiques. The McGregor Mall is open seven days a week, 10 to 5; in other shops, the hours and days open vary.

McGregor has a lot to offer in addition to antiques. The area has some important historical sites including early Native American mounds. It's close to a landing for a riverboat gambling casino, and the active chamber of commerce makes sure that there are always interesting weekend events during the summer.

TO GET THERE: McGregor is just across the river from the much larger Prairie du Chien, Wisconsin, another early traders' town. Take Scenic Highway 60 west from Wisconsin through Prairie du Chien and across the Mississippi River, or Scenic Highway 76 east through Iowa.

FOR MORE INFORMATION: McGregor Chamber of Commerce, telephone 1-800-896-0910.

KANSAS

Wichita Mid-America Flea Market

This large flea market, which often has as many as 650 vendors, is open September through June on one Sunday each month. Because the site is the Kansas Coliseum, the date isn't always the same every month. Call for the next month's date before you travel. This market has a large following; it's been in business for 18 years here.

TO GET THERE: Exit 17 off Interstate 135, at the junction of 85th Street North and the interstate.

FOR MORE INFORMATION: Write Mid-America at P.O. Box 1585, Hutchinson, KS 67504 or telephone 1-316-663-5626.

ADDENDUM: Mid-America also operates an antiques market in Hutchinson, Kansas, the firm's home base, on the first Sunday of every month, October through June. It's located at the Kansas State Fairgrounds at 20th and Main. Other good places to look for antiques in this state are in the small towns of Fall River, on Route 96, and Chanute, on Route 169, in the southeastern part of the state.

MISSOURI

Branson and Environs

The explosive growth of Branson, Missouri, into a major musical attraction that features country music stars who perform in their own theaters, has had an equally dramatic affect on the antiques market in the southwestern part of the state.

Suddenly, within the past few years, the Branson area has become an antiques mecca. With six million people drawn to this area, antiques shops and malls have been opening almost as fast as the theaters have been selling tickets.

Crystal and Leland Payton are residents of nearby Springfield, Missouri, twenty-five miles from Branson, who buy and sell antiques as well as write about them. Crystal also writes travel books including the *Insider's Guide to Branson and the Ozark Mountains* (Insider's Guide, Inc., Manteo, NC, 1995).

They say the antiques shops and malls in Branson are more attractive to tourists looking for souvenirs than to the antiques aficionado because a lot of the merchandise is reproduction.

But the small towns and highways leading into Branson are full of interesting shops that offer the kind of rich assortment of antiques you might expect to find in a major city.

Cheri Russell, "The Wicker Fixer," also publishes a detailed area map that lists most of the shops in Branson and its surrounding communities. She says nearby Springfield's antiques community has great picking potential, particularly in the three malls—Springfield Antique Company, South Peer, and Jerry's, all within a few feet of each other in downtown Springfield.

Bass Country Emporium, specializing in vintage hunting and fishing equipment, is also located in Springfield, as is the one-hundred-dealer Old Town Antique Mall and Flea Market, the Coach House, and the Century Art Gallery, a mini-mall.

Ozark, Missouri, ten miles south of Springfield as you head toward Branson, may be even more rewarding; it is chock-full of small shops and malls, including the new 160-dealer dealer Ozark Antiques, located with several other malls at the junction of US 65 and State Highway 14.

TO GET THERE: From Springfield, take US 65 south through Ozark to Branson.

FOR MORE INFORMATION: Cheri Russell will send you a copy of her antiques dealers' map free of charge if you send her an SASE. Write to her at 924 Prairie Ridge Rd., Ozark, MO, 65721

NEBRASKA

Buffalo County Antique Flea Market

Promoter Cynthia Svarvari says that Helen Robinson of the Illinois Kane County show is her mentor. (The Kearney, Nebraska woman says that she sold for 12 years at the Chicago area show, six of them outside during the winter cold and snow before she had enough longevity to qualify for an indoor spot.)

Using the knowledge she had gathered during her stint in Illinois, she founded her own show four years ago, and now brings 104 dealers, 95% of them antiques and collectibles vendors, together four times a year in Kearney. She also does shows in nearby Lexington, Nebraska, and in Columbus, Nebraska. These markets are a good place to look for country primitive furniture and farm collectibles.

TO GET THERE: Kearney is located less than two miles north of Interstate 80 in the center of the state.
FOR MORE INFORMATION: Write to 403 9th Street, Overton, Nebraska, 68863, or telephone 1-308-987-2633.

OKLAHOMA

May Antique Mall

Oklahoma City has quite a few antiques shops and malls, most clustered in the City's downtown area along or near May Street. The May Mall is the largest in the downtown area with 85 dealers who offer a little of everything. The May Mall, located in an old theater building, is open Monday through Saturday year-round.

There's also a flea market every weekend with both indoor and outdoor booths that can have as many as 500 vendors; many, but not all, sell antiques and collectibles.

TO GET THERE: Take Interstate 40 to the Pennsylvania exit, then Pennsylvania Avenue north. The shops are clustered around 10th to 23rd Street between Pennsylvania and May. The AMC flea market is at 1001 North Pennsylvania Avenue.

FOR MORE INFORMATION: May Antique Mall, 1515 No. May, Oklahoma City, OK 73107 or telephone 1-405-947-3800.

ARKANSAS

Eureka Springs

A small town with only 2,000 residents, Eureka Springs is nevertheless a fascinating community that attracts thousands of tourists every year. They're drawn by the abundance of picturesque streets and carefully preserved Victorian buildings. Many of the buildings in the town's business loop which encircles the community are listed in the National Register of Historic Landmarks. Not surprisingly, many are also antiques shops—23 at last count, a lot for a small community. Several are malls, but most of the shops here are independently owned.

Although the dealers in Eureka Springs sell a wide range of antiques, this is an extremely good place to look for folk art, especially Ozark art, as it's known, which most dealers like to feature in their shops.

Folk art and antiques are the focus at a spring festival held every year at the War Eagle Mill, an old grist mill just outside of town, and in November,

Eureka Springs hosts an antique show featuring dealers from nine states.

TO GET THERE: Eureka Springs is in the northwestern corner of the state, close to the Missouri border, about an hour away from Branson. Take Route 62W which goes right into the town.

FOR MORE INFORMATION: Jane and David Baker own Springs Antiques and also produce the annual November antiques show. Write to them at 6 So. Main St., Eureka Springs, AR 72632 or telephone 1-501-253-7551; for a map of antiques shops and calendar of events, contact the Eureka Springs Chamber of Commerce at 81 Kings Highway, Eureka Springs, AR 72632, telephone 1-501-253-7333.

ADDENDUM: Other good places to hunt for antiques in Arkansas are the town of Hot Springs, just south and west of Little Rock, the state capital, as well as Ft. Smith and Van Buren, close to the Oklahoma border.

CHAPTER ELEVEN

REALLY EASY REPAIRS

Like in real estate, the biggest antiques bargains usually are the fixer-uppers. Even if you have absolutely no flair for doing handiwork, there are some extremely easy repairs that can make you feel that you've done your bit of spinning straw into gold because you can increase the value of something you own by tenfold in a matter of hours. I've seen pieces in malls and flea markets marked at a mere fraction of their value just because one drawer pull is missing from a bureau, for example, or the glass in a mirror needs to be replaced.

Then there are the more esoteric repairs, simple to do but requiring some kind of hard-to-find part. If you look through Chapter Nineteen, you'll find resources for almost every kind of antiques replacement part you may need, from reproduction painted lampshades for those expensive hanging lamps to brass turkey claw feet for a piano stool or curved glass for a picture frame.

The most common defect in an antique is dirt, the decades of dirt and grease that become part of the finish on furniture, or turn linens into ugly graying and yellowing rags.

There are some fairly intense debates going on within the antiques world right now over whether it's appropriate to do any kind of restoration or repair at all. Conservators at museums say you should never do any kind of repair that's irreversible. If you're going to fix it up, you should always be able to return it to its original condition.

While this may be true in some cases, in other situations it's just plain silly. I once heard a linen conservator advance the argument that antique cloth should be left in the condition in which it was found, no matter how revolting. That means you could never use that hand-embroidered tablecloth because no one could eat off it in its disgustingly stained and grayed condition.

So, a little common sense is called for here. Obviously, if Picasso doodled on a restaurant table cloth, you're not going to want to bleach out the pen and ink sketches. But, if all Picasso did was spill pea soup on that tablecloth, it's perfectly proper to clean it up so it can be used again. Most of us who buy antiques want to find a place for them in our daily lives, and it's awfully difficult to live with dirt, no matter how genuinely antique it, too, may be.

The first rule of repair is: try soap and water. Mix your solution, according to package or bottle directions, sponge it on, and then quickly dry the surface with old absorbent towels if you have them, or paper towels if you don't. Try not to let water sit on a surface, ever, and proceed cautiously. If you're washing a piece of wooden furniture that has been veneered, standing water can soak through the thin veneer and it will begin to rise like a bubble. Sponge a small, inconspicuous spot first to see what happens before you start to splash water over the entire piece.

You can use a mild, all-purpose cleaner like Murphy's Oil Soap, which will remove a lot of grunge on almost any hard surface. Murphy's now also makes a stronger kitchen cleaner that's very effective as well. For a primitive furniture piece in very rough condition—say something that's been sitting in the back of a barn for fifty years—I use a strong solution of Spic and Span.

Vinegar almost always will eliminate any kind of odor, even those associated with dogs or cats, and usually won't affect wood or other hard surfaces adversely. If you run into a really tough odor problem, there's a vinegar concentrate sold in supermarkets that's even better, and for the very worst odors, try Massingil's Douche in the original formula. Put it in a spray bottle, spray the entire surface, drawer, or cupboard interior, and let it dry. Keep drawers or doors closed for a day.

I was surprised to learn that a lot of dealers who specialize in linens and laces don't hesitate to use a little bleach to get delicate fabrics clean. They use a weak solution, never let the piece stay in it for very long, and rinse carefully and thoroughly.

I don't mind tossing cottons or linens into bleach, but you can run into big trouble if you're trying to wash silk, particularly old silk, which can shatter into fine strips of nothing if you're not careful. Once, because I was in a hurry and stupidly careless, I took a genuine collar frill, that ascot-like bit of netting or lace the founding fathers wore back in the eighteenth century, and dunked it in a bleach solution. It promptly dissolved into disaster.

Ivory Snow soap flakes, which used to be non-detergent, were a favorite with dealers because detergents can be too harsh and unpredictable when they come into contact with fabric. Now, unfortunately, Ivory Snow does have detergent in it, so if you feel the piece you need to clean is far too delicate to wash without special attention, you can look for a quilt wash called Ensure, distributed by Mountain Mist and available through conservation supply catalogs or sometimes in pharmacies.

If you're trying to fix up an old quilt, the most important thing to remember is never to patch an old quilt with new fabric. You can usually find bits of old fabric in antiques shops, or shards of old quilts to help you repair one that is damaged.

Never, ever, dry clean a quilt. Museum conservators clean them by vacuuming them carefully with a small upholstery vacuum attachment, using a fine mesh screen as a buffer between the vacuum suction and the cloth itself.

If some of the pieces in a quilt have shattered—you see this a lot with crazy quilts, those Victorian quilts that were made from odd scraps of fragile fabrics like silk—you can cover and preserve the spot that's corroding with something called crepeline. This is a nearly invisible fabric that comes in several very neutral shades. You can apply it on top of the damaged fabric to hold the remains in place. It, too, can be ordered from museum supply houses. (See Chapter Nineteen.)

Some quilt experts actually recommend washing badly soiled and stained quilts made from cotton fabrics, and otherwise in sound condition, in the washing machine. I tried this once and believe me, it wasn't pretty. The quilt came out in wads of ripped fabric and batting and was damaged so badly that I couldn't even make a throw pillow out of any of it.

So, I would take that particular bit of "expert" advice with a grain of salt.

One dealer I know has been very successful in washing quilts in the bathtub, soaking them in a solution of liquid dishwasher detergent and cool water. I tried this, too, and it does seem to work, but count on having the bathtub remain out of commission for several days. You have to soak the quilt overnight and then spend several days rinsing and soaking to get the soap scum out of it. I wound up treading barefoot on my quilt to rinse it, the way they stomp on all those grapes in Sardinia.

Then, when you've gotten as much water out of the quilt as you can without twisting and wringing, spread the quilt out on the lawn flat, or over some strong bushes, and keep it out of direct sunlight so it doesn't fade. Do this early in the day when the humidity is low, and it will be dry or close to dry by night fall and you can easily bring it inside.

A lot of otherwise good quilts are damaged around the edges and there's a fairly simple cure for this problem, too. Trim off the frayed edges and bind them with a wide or narrow strip of complementary fabric, cut on the bias for flexibility. Hand stitch this binding in place. You can use new fabric here but to make it blend in more naturally with the quilt, wash it three or four times in your washer first. If you want to fade it just a little, add bleach. Or, if you soak the binding in tea water, you'll get a faintly aged look. Make a quart or so of tea just the way you would if you were planning to drink it and allow the binding to soak in it for ten minutes or so.

If you encounter rust on linens, there is a rust remover on the market that will take out spots without taking the fabric with it. It's called Whink and you can buy it in the hardware store. Follow directions, and test first before you get carried away.

The debate over original condition versus usefulness gets a lot louder when furniture is the subject of discussion. Here, even dealers who usually line up on the side of a little quick bleach and spray starch for their linens suddenly take the opposite side of the debate and start talking about the integrity of a piece, telling customers to leave the original finish alone.

There's a fairly practical reason for this. Leaving furniture in its original painted condition saves a lot of work for dealers, who only a few years ago were either stripping all antique furniture themselves to get that light, bare wood look, or sending it off to expensive refinishers who did it for them.

While it is now fashionable to leave a painted surface alone, or even to enhance its age by painting it with special surface conditioners that create a crackled look, this is not a hard-and-fast rule.

A lot of painted surfaces are not that old or interesting and certainly don't need to be preserved. Recently I saw a fantastic old blanket chest, definitely eighteenth century. It was wearing a coat of that acid-y yellow-green that was so popular in the early seventies and it was godawful. Were I to buy this blanket chest, the first thing I'd do would be to strip it back to whatever's underneath.

Sometimes you can find an original painted surface under a relatively modern coat of paint. If you want to try to restore that original coat of paint, first consult a furniture restorer. Often, scraping the top coat of paint off with razor blades is the only way to keep the original paint underneath intact. It takes a lot of time and a lot of razor blades. I've only done it with one piece—a six-board blanket chest, and the end result was definitely worth it. I'd work on it in spare moments and it took me about a year.

But if you're dealing with something that's been painted baby-bottom pink, another great thirties color, I don't think you have to worry about preserving it for posterity. Go ahead and strip it.

And if you are looking at a piece of furniture with a beautiful old original finish that you absolutely hate? I once considered buying a wonderful old Welsh cupboard, in pine, but with original paint the color of mustard that's dried on a plate, a shade I can't stand. My solution? I just didn't buy it. I didn't want to ruin the piece and somewhere else in the world there's a person who probably loves that color and will keep the cupboard just that way.

If you do decide to strip a piece of furniture, use the old-fashioned, lung-rotting type of stripper, and use it outdoors where it will do the least amount of damage to you. There are a lot of new strippers out that are less dangerous, but they're less effective as well.

Buy the semi-paste, never the liquid, because you'll use a lot less of it. Work in one small area at a time—one side of a bureau, or just the top. After applying the stripper with an old brush, cover the part you've just painted with clear plastic wrap or wax paper. This intensifies the action of the stripper and you won't have to apply as many coats.

You will soon learn whether you like to strip furniture or not. It doesn't seem to be a chore that allows a lukewarm response. People either love doing it or give up in the middle of the first piece and start looking for a commercial refinisher.

If you get into refinishing, watch out for the painted oak finish that appears on a lot of turn-of-the-century pieces. This finish, which was applied with something that looked very much like today's paint rollers, duplicated the look of quarter-sawed oak, highly popular back then. It darkens with time and now looks remarkably like genuine oak with a coat of old varnish covering the grain.

Once I started to strip a bureau and watched in horror as the oak graining itself began to disappear. Shocked, I kept throwing more paint stripper on the bureau, and scrubbing at it harder with steel wool, hoping to bring back the "oak" surface, until I finally realized that the oak look had been painted on and was never going to return.

If all you need to do to clean up a piece of furniture is to remove the old, dirty varnish, mix denatured alcohol and lacquer thinner together in equal amounts and apply it with a paintbrush. Immediately wipe off any residue with fine steel wool. Work in one small area at a time and finish with a coat of wax.

There are also purists who feel that polishing brass or silver is wrong, as is replacing old mirror with new. In fact, there are now chemicals available that will give your bright, new mirror some of the cloudy, crackled, and darkened quality that old mirrors acquire after time.

There's an easy way to give old mirror glass functionality of a new mirror, while keeping the look of the old. If the original mirror is worth preserving because it has wide beveled borders, for instance, you can remove the mirror finish from the back with bleach, or with furniture stripper, and wash it down until you are left with a piece of clear glass. Set it back into the mirror frame and then, right behind it, mount a piece of thin mirror glass, the thinnest you can get, cut to the same size. The new mirror will look as though it's part of the old glass.

If you like the look of shiny brass and copper, a bathroom cleaner called Scrub-free works better than any metal cleaner on the market. Soak drawer pulls or knobs in it, or for larger surfaces, spritz it on straight from the bottle and then rub with very fine 0000-grade steel wool. Buff when it dries. Your brass will be beautiful and you won't have to clean it as often. I have a brass bed I clean this way, and rather than having to clean in three or four times a year, I now do it once, in much less time than it used to take.

Scrub-Free works on copper, too, but it doesn't seem to be very effective on silver or silverplate. For that you need Nevr-Dull, a product that almost all antiques dealers have tucked in their cupboard. You tear off a tiny piece of treated cotton wad that comes in a can and tarnish disappears with a couple of swipes.

Another really great product that almost every antiques dealer uses is Briwax. Originally formulated for use at the British Museum, this combination wax and cleaner works on leather, wood, and even some metals. The Briwax Light Brown is the finish you see most often on stripped furniture. Put a couple of coats on with fine steel wool, buff if you want a gleaming finish or leave it alone if you prefer a mat look, and you're finished.

Wobbly legs on a table or chair are easy to fix as well. Don't expect to cure the problem by regluing. Often, old chair rungs or joints have loosened because wood cells shrink with age. The solution is to wrap a loose-fitting chair rung with fine thread before you fit it in place, and then glue, or if you can't pull the rung out or get into a joint, shove glue-soaked wooden toothpicks into the open space until the wiggle is gone. Use a straight razor to cut off the toothpicks at the woodline so they don't show.

There are two important things to remember about any kind of glue job: 1) Always remove every trace of old glue before you glue again, and 2) apply pressure by weighting or clamping or the glue won't hold, no matter what the package directions say.

Most of the time, wood repairs can be made with plain old carpenter's wood glue, manufactured by a number of companies. There is another type of wood glue, a powder that mixes with water, that will create a stronger bond. Dealers don't use it too often because once you've glued, you've Glued. The wood will never come apart at that particular spot again, and that can mean that if another break occurs, the piece will be impossible to fix. Better to leave yourself some room, so that if you do have to take apart a table or chair, you can. Regular wood glue will dissolve with hot water, or, in tough cases, hot water mixed with vinegar.

If your problem is a piece of wobbly old wicker, you can correct that with glue, too. Mix one part white glue with one part cool water. Turn the wicker piece upside down and spray the solution into every crack and corner, getting as much to soak into the wicker as you can. Let it dry overnight without moving it and repeat the next day. Repaint when the wicker is completely dry.

Drop leaf tables, table leaves, and drawer fronts often warp if they've been exposed to the elements or left in a damp place. You can get the warp out of wood so easily it almost seems like magic. You're going to need a hot, sunny day, so don't try this in winter. Take your warped board outside early in the morning when the grass is still wet with dew and lay it on a flat spot of lawn in the sun, concave side facing down.

That's it. That's all there is to it. Leave it alone until the warp straightens out. That may take anywhere from a few hours to a few days, depending upon the density of the wood. You can speed up the process a little by dousing the section of lawn you're going to use with a bucket of hot water first.

When the board is straight, bring it back inside. Sometimes, the warp will return, although it never will be as bad. If this happens, repeat the outdoor treatment again. Eventually the wood will get tired of fighting back and stay straight.

Wood veneer can warp or bubble on a table or bureau surface when water loosens the glue that holds this thin layer of wood to the actual surface. You can cure this with an ordinary iron. Place a cloth over the spot to protect the finish, turn the iron to medium heat, and iron over the warp or bubble until it disappears. If the surface doesn't smooth out immediately, dampen the cloth or switch your iron to its steam setting and try that.

A veneer surface that's badly damaged doesn't always mean that the piece is irreparable. A lot of those round oak tables, for example, had oak veneer on top of, guess what, solid oak. All you have to do is pull off the oak veneer by soaking it with hot water and vinegar, and then using a putty knife to loosen and remove it in sections. When the veneer is off, refinish the new surface by sanding and staining or waxing.

Chipped china? All it takes is one of those wonderful boxes of crayons with all the colors. Find the crayon closest to the shade you need to match and melt a little with a match or lighter. Drip the melting wax into the chip until it disappears. You can smooth the surface with your finger while the wax is wet, sand it lightly with an emery board for a mat finish, or buff it to a shiny surface if you want. And if you're really compulsive, you can try blending a couple of crayons together to get a perfect match, although this isn't usually necessary.

When you want to reglue broken pieces of china, you'll need a second pair of hands to help. Glue both broken edges, and fit them together carefully, working as a team. One person holds the two parts together, acting as a human clamp while the second adjusts the fit until the break is almost invisible.

Wait until the glue has set—the glue package directions will tell you how long—and then carefully set the piece in a box of loose sand, or bank it with small, sand-filled bags so that the break is supported. Leave it alone for a couple of days.

If you need to fill in a broken spot on a ceramic or plaster figure, you can use an old-fashioned plaster bandage called Unna's Boot Dressing. Cut or wrap it to fill in the damaged spots or reattach a broken segment.

If you have a friendly dentist, like mine—Dr. John

Pitman in Tenafly, New Jersey, who tells me he's used dental clay and acrylic to fix everything from the fuel pump in his car to fine porcelain—take advantage of his or her kindness and get some of the products dentists use. The clay they use to take impressions is extremely useful in reproducing small bits of the elaborate plaster trim you want to replace on one part of a picture frame. Make a mold from an intact section of the frame with the clay and then fill it with plaster of paris. Fit the remade section by shaping it with a knife. You can also use dental acrylic to fill and sculpt missing sections of picture frames or any other multidimensional object. Dental tools are also great to have handy when you're repairing almost anything. They're extremely versatile and designed for use on small surfaces. Your dentist can even help you order surgeon's gloves of disposable, but sturdy, close-fitting latex.

Don't Try This at Home: Repairs That Require Special Equipment or Skills

Chair backs and vertical slats. You're looking for real trouble when you try to re-glue these parts of a chair, because they receive extra pressure when they're in use. Take them to a good repair shop and see if there is anything they can do.

Rockers. When rockers go, it looks as though it ought to be easy to re-glue them. Not so. The rocker also receives pressure and usually breaks again very quickly. Buy replacement rockers from any of the antiques supply stores or swap them out with another old rocker that's too tired to fix up. Make sure they're the same size as the originals.

Rips and tears in prints and paintings. You can do more harm that good if you try to make these repairs on your own. If you're determined to proceed because professional repairs are too pricey, buy books and videos or take a course first.

Replating silver plate. Magazines often advertise tubes of silver that will redo silver plate and make your old Victorian butter dish shine. It doesn't seem to work very well. If you want a piece replated, take it to a department store with a silver department. Often these stores have an annual sale on replating.

Cutting down picture frames. This is one of those projects that looks as though it ought to be awfully easy but isn't. You can't just use a miter box and saw to recut a frame and expect it to come back together easily. No one I know has ever successfully changed the size of a frame without special tools to hold the newly shaped frame while you glue and fill in the gaps with wood filler.

CHAPTER TWELVE

MIDWEST REGION

Indiana, Illinois, Minnesota, Michigan, Ohio, Wisconsin

INDIANA

Shipshewana

This mammoth auction is one of the best places in the country to buy antiques at bargain prices. I'd rate it one of the top ten.

Every Wednesday, starting at 8:00 A.M., at least a dozen or perhaps as many as fifty auctioneers conduct simultaneous sales in a huge metal building. There are no paddles, no numbers, no seats. Buyers can register in advance in the auction office to be able to pay by check or credit card there, or pay cash to the individual auctioneers as they roam the huge room.

Auctioneers stand by their respective groups of

goods and shout into handheld electronic micro-
phones while buyers gather around in a more or less
attentive circle. There's nothing to compel you to
stay through any auction to its conclusion; in fact,
almost no one does. Wait for the merchandise on
which you'd like to bid to come up, and then wander
off somewhere else.

As you can imagine, the noise of dozens of people
talking and bidding and shouting, added to the com-
bined choir of auctioneers' voices, creates a truly ter-
rible din in the metal building. I saw a lot of dealers
who were wearing earplugs. When they wanted to
bid on an item, they'd remove the earplugs until that
particular lot was sold; then they'd put the plugs
back in again.

Shipshewana opens its doors for inspection at 6:00
A.M. You will really want to be there the moment
the doors open. In the noisy chaos that ensues when
the auctions all start, it's almost impossible to focus
on seriously checking out the merchandise you want
to buy.

Don't try to drive long distances overnight to get
to this auction, either. You're much better off if you
check into a nearby motel—Elkhart is full of them
and it's about a half hour away—the night before.

The bargains, if you can ignore the distractions
and focus on the bidding, can be remarkable. I saw
beautiful old spoon-carved shelves selling for $35; a
spinning wheel in perfect condition for $75, and doz-
ens of bureaus going for less than $100. A lot of

dealers arrive here with a big truck, bid until the auction closes in early afternoon, and leave with enough stock to carry them for months.

Not that everything is pure gold. Those goat/dog/hay/grape carts that are such clever reproductions are sold here. One dealer from Chicago who attends these auctions every week told me that these carts never sell for less than $175 here because the creators have a shill in place who won't let them go for less. Not only are these carts fakes, they're price-fixed!

Dealers also warn against trying to attend these auctions during the peak summer months unless you're a complete masochist. When you combine as many as four thousands buyers and sellers under one hot tin roof in July, you can imagine the temperature inside the building.

Flea markets operate outside the building in the summer and in an adjacent building year-round. Shipshewana is open every Wednesday except for the two-week period that encompasses Christmas and New Year's.

There is a restaurant, somewhat unappetizingly called the Pork Haus, on the auction premises, but because the area is filled with plain people sects (you'll see lots of horses and buggies on the roads) there are great restaurants offering hearty meals nearby. The 5 and 20, a restaurant so named because it's located at the intersection of Route 5 and Route 20, is inexpensive and wonderful.

TO GET THERE: Route 20 east from South Bend to Route 5, then south on 5 to Shipshewana. You can't miss it; it's right on the road.

FOR MORE INFORMATION: Telephone 1-219-768-4129

Napanee

About an hour's drive from the auction, heading south and then west on Route 6, is the small town of Napanee, filled to the brim with antiques malls. I suspect that most of the mall merchandise comes from Shipshewana or other, smaller auctions in the area. I saw some very good country primitive cupboards at extremely reasonable prices and some quite ornate bureaus that seemed inexpensive, too.

There's also an auction in Napanee, every Tuesday at 8:00 A.M., at the Dutch Village Mall and Marketplace, located on County Road 101, just north of US Highway 6, 1^1/$_2$ miles west of State Road 19.

TO GET THERE: Follow Route 6, which parallels Route 20 to the south. Napanee is just after the intersection of Route 6 and Highway 15.

FOR MORE INFORMATION: Napanee Antique Mall, telephone 1-219-773-3278; Dutch Village, 1-219-773-2828, ask for Joe.

ILLINOIS

Kane County Flea Market

In 1967, Helen Robinson started her flea market here at the county fairgrounds with 14 dealers. Today her monthly weekend antiques and collectibles show is rated one of the top markets in the country, and the 1,200 to 1,500 dealers who gather here on the first Sunday of the month and its preceding Saturday attract at least 30,000 people every weekend. Indoor and outdoor booths are open year round, no matter what the weather.

Dealers from every state in the country have sold here at one time or another, and the market is now so well known that it has become a regular travel stop for European visitors.

Admission is $4; parking and children are free.

TO GET THERE: The market is located in St. Charles, about 40 miles west of Chicago. Take Route 64 to Randal Road.

FOR MORE INFORMATION: Telephone 1-630-377-2252.

MINNESOTA

John Kruesel's General Merchandise

John Kruesel is a purist, a dealer who not only loves antiques but sees as his mission in life their preservation and protection. A former president of the local historical society, he operates his small store in the town of Rochester, Minnesota, which is known primarily as the location of the Mayo Clinic.

Kruesel's shop is filled with the kind of eighteenth- and nineteenth-century furniture that is so increasingly hard to find. Even as a dealer, he says he has trouble acquiring pieces that are top quality and in fine condition. He doesn't like to handle pieces that he describes as "make do" and he won't stock anything that is less than authentic.

His store is also the place to go if you're looking for genuine period lighting fixtures. Kruesel is so knowledgeable about Early American lighting that he is called on regularly to consult on special restorations. Recently he was brought to New York City to oversee the lighting restoration in the first Jewish synagogue ever built here. (He went home and wrote a two hundred-page dissertation about it.)

Conversation with Kruesel is a college course in itself. He can talk in great detail about the different kinds of lamp fuel used in earlier times. Did you know that only affluent people used whale oil in their lamps? Poor people used smokier, smellier lard. In the nineteenth century, a volatile mixture of turpentine and alcohol was fashionable, until too many explosions and fires discouraged its use.

Kruesel is also an expert on vintage plumbing, although he doesn't like to deal much in it anymore. He is one of the very few people in this country who has a copper bathtub that folds up into the wall much like an early bed. This nineteenth-century wonder was concealed by an elaborate oak door, which also concealed a kerosene hot water heater.

TO GET THERE: Take Interstate 90 to Highway 63, north eight miles. Kruesel is located at 22 Third St. Southwest, Rochester, MN, 55902

FOR MORE INFORMATION: Telephone 1-507-289-8049

Gold Rush Days

There are two Gold Rush events in Minnesota. The Rochester festival of antiques takes place three times a year—the second weekend in May, the third weekend in August, and the last weekend in September. During each of these events, 1,400 dealers gather at the Olmsted County Fairgrounds and offer a wide range of antiques and collectibles at bargain prices over 52 acres of indoor and outdoor booths.

The Rochester event is an outgrowth of the Oronoco Gold Rush, a community-wide antiques sale that occurs on a weekend in mid-August. Oronoco, which is about 10 miles from Rochester, allows the 1,000 participating dealers to set up their booths throughout the downtown Oronoco area. Dealer fees from this show go to community projects.

TO GET THERE: Take Interstate 90 to Highway 63 to Rochester. Oronoco is 10 miles north on Highway 82.

FOR MORE INFORMATION: Write to Box 266, Oronoco, MN 55960, or call 507-367-4400; for Rochester call 507-288-0320.

Red Wing

This town comes by its designation as an antiques center rightfully, because it's here that the famous Red Wing Pottery began production. Today, there are seventeen antiques shops and malls in the small town with a total of approximately 300 dealers. Al's Antique Mall, with 100 dealer spaces, will supply a free map of all the antiques locations in town.

TO GET THERE: Red Wing is about 50 miles south of Minneapolis on Route 61.

FOR MORE INFORMATION: Write to Al's Antique Mall, 1314 Old West Main St., Red Wing, MN 55066, or telephone 1-612-388-0572.

ADDENDUM: If you go to Red Wing, you might as well drive a few miles further to the riverfront town of Stillwater, also an antiquers delight because it's filled with shops.

MICHIGAN

Caravan Antiques Market

This popular 500-dealer show is held five times a year, in May, June, July, August and October on

Sundays, for one day only. It's located in the almost nonexistent hamlet of Centreville, located south of Kalamazoo at the southern edge of the state just a few miles north of the Indiana border.

Because this show is located in the heart of Amish country, lots of the mom and pop dealers who show here have great primitives to sell. Pickers love to come here, because this show has such a well-established reputation for being the site of great bargains. The show opens officially at 7 A.M. but by that time traffic is backed up for miles, so try to get there much earlier if you can.

TO GET THERE: The show is located at the St. Joseph's County Fairgrounds in Centreville; take Route 131 south from Kalamazoo or north from Interstate 80, get off at State Highway 86.

FOR MORE INFORMATION: Telephone, 1-313-227-4464.

Ann Arbor Antiques Market

For 28 years, the Ann Arbor Antiques Market has been offering a monthly antiques show that features quality dealers in antiques and collectibles. There is a vetting process, to make sure all antiques sold as such are authentic.

The indoor market is open Saturdays and Sundays one weekend each month from May through November. Dates vary. Admission $4.

TO GET THERE: Interstate 94 east or west, or US Route 23 north or south.

FOR MORE INFORMATION: Write to P.O. Box 1512, Ann Arbor, Michigan 48106, or telephone 1-313-662-9453.

OHIO

Springfield Antique Show and Flea Market

Billed as the largest and best market in the midwest, Springfield is a huge show that normally attracts around 1,200 dealers every month. Most of them come from the surrounding eight states, but there are also dealers from both coasts and most points in-between, especially during the three-day extravaganzas, when the dealer population swells to 2,500 or more.

Open Saturdays and Sundays year-round, except for extravaganza weekends, when buyers can shop on Fridays during dealer set-up for $5. Admission, $2 daily, $3 for extravaganzas.

TO GET THERE: Interstate 70 to Exit 59, to the Clark County Fairgrounds.

FOR MORE INFORMATION: Write to P.O. Box 2429, Springfield, Ohio 45501 or telephone 1-513-325-0053.

Valley View Expo Center and Antique Mall

This huge mall—173,000 sq. ft. with 80,000 sq. ft. devoted to antiques and collectibles—is one of the largest antiques malls in the country. There are 300 dealer booths as well as another 144 showcases and the center is expanding rapidly.

Open seven days a week, with a "superswap" flea market and farm produce market on Tuesdays where anything and everything from boats to bureaus is brought in for sale.

TO GET THERE: Interstate 80 to Exit 234, at the Pennsylvania border. Take Route 7 north three miles to Brookfield center, turn right on Warren-Sharon Road. **FOR MORE INFORMATION:** Write to 7281 Warren-Sharon Road, Brookfield, Ohio 44403, or telephone 1-800-587-2535.

Riverfront Antique Mall

This large 84,000 sq. ft. one-floor mall has more than 350 participating dealers, and features fine antiques and collectibles as well as a "rough room" where bargain hunters can look for fixer-uppers. Open seven days.

TO GET THERE: Take Interstate 77 to Exit 81, then State Highway 39 east to the first traffic light, turn right and follow to the mall.

FOR MORE INFORMATION: 1203 Front Ave., SW, New Philadelphia, Ohio 44663, or telephone 1-800-926-9806

WISCONSIN

Maxwell Street Days

Five times each summer, the small town of Cedarburg, Wisconsin, becomes the site for Maxwell Street Days. In this suburb of Milwaukee, anything and everything on the picturesque streets is sold from farm produce fresh from the fields and handed out off the backs of trucks to fine glassware or primitive antiques.

The event is named after Chicago's famous Maxwell Street, a bargain area in that city. Proceeds from the booth and space rental go to community projects.

Cedarburg sponsors a number of community wide events during the course of the year, including a spectacular Christmas celebration that turns the streets, and the old mill that is one of the town's primary attractions (and filled with antiques shops), into an old-fashioned wonderland.

TO GET THERE: Cedarburg is just north of Milwaukee on the Lake Michigan shoreline. Interstate 43 goes right into the town.

FOR MORE INFORMATION: Maxwell Street Days, 1-414-377-8412, Special events, 1-414-377-5856.

Rummage-O-Rama

As many as 600 sellers converge on West Allis, a southwestern suburb of Milwaukee one weekend each month for this indoor market that has a little bit of everything. It is a favorite place for dealers to look for antiques.

TO GET THERE: Rummage-O-Rama is held at the State Fairgrounds off Route 94, the East-West Freeway.
FOR MORE INFORMATION: Telephone 1-414-521-2111

Broadway Antique Mall

This 60-dealer mall in the college town of Madison was voted the best antique shop in the state by a Wisconsin magazine last year. There's a huge carpeted showroom for furniture and small objects, as well as a large "rough room" for bargain hunters. Open seven days.

TO GET THERE: Take Interstate 90 to the Madison beltline to the Monona Drive exit.
FOR MORE INFORMATION: Write to 115 Broadway, Madison, WI 53716
ADDENDUM: Wisconsin dealers love to hunt for an-

tiques in the northern part of the state, where there
are small bargain-filled shops and great rural auctions. Check out Wisconsin Rapids, Rhinelander
and Wausau.

CHAPTER THIRTEEN

WHAT'S IT WORTH?

Want to know the single most often repeated sentence in the antiques world, the one dealers hear on an almost daily basis as customers browse through their shops? It's—"Oh, my God! We took one just like that to the dump!"

The reason this cry resounds so regularly is directly attributable to the change in popular attitudes toward antiques.

For most average families in this country, until very recently, old stuff used to be considered faintly shameful. If you were still using grandma's furniture, you were considered to be living a hand-me-down existence that indicated you hadn't yet made enough of a mark in the world to be able to furnish your home with everything that was new and shiny. The exceptions to the belief that new was always better might be a few treasured heirlooms—the family Bible or picture album, perhaps a christening gown or a lace tablecloth.

This attitude hasn't entirely dissipated, especially in some of the more rural sections of the country, thankfully, so those of us who love to hunt for antiques can still manage once in a while to turn up something fairly toothsome.

Until recently, the person with an educated antiques eye, who was knowledgeable enough about antiques to stroll confidently into an auction or shop and buy with certainty, was almost invariably wealthy, well-educated, and upper class.

Now, of course, that's changed. Collectors number in the millions and they cut across every imaginable age group and strata of society.

If you could have a bird's-eye view of the United States on any Saturday morning when the weather's behaving, you'd be able to see hundreds of thousands of cars zipping along back roads and down highways to get to the next yard sale, the next auction or antique mall or show, all in hot pursuit of whatever it is they consider treasure.

Today, most of these people are becoming as knowledgeable as that rarified group of well-bred experts who used to dominate the antiques collecting arena.

As one rather grumpy dealer, who used to stock booths in five different malls and now can maintain only two, complained, "You used to be able to make a fairly good living at this, traveling around, getting things cheap, and selling them through the malls, but now it's all changed. There's a lot more competition because all the housewives have gotten in on it."

If there are still people around who don't want grandma's old stuff, most of them now know that there is value in what were once considered worthless discards.

But there's a lot of distance between being able to generally tell the difference between a fake and an authentic piece, and having the kind of detailed, specific knowledge that allows you to recognize a real treasure instantly.

I know a dealer who's a sort of American version of Lovejoy, at least in terms of his ability to sniff out great antiques.

To give you an idea—just a few weeks ago, he wandered into a yard sale and picked up a Japanese inro for $25 dollars. An inro, you ask? What's that? Well, you've probably heard of netsukes, those carved ivory or wooden figures that hang from a cord looped over a kimono belt. The whole purpose of a netsuke was to anchor an inro, which is a small Japanese purse that hangs at the other end of the cord holding the netsuke. The netsuke acts as a counterweight to the purse, keeping it firmly in place.

Had I been at that same yard sale, I wouldn't have known what it was, and apparently neither did anyone else who was there that day because the inro he picked up for $25 is worth thousands.

Maddeningly, he does this all the time.

He insists on being anonymous, but he was willing to share some of his expertise.

How does he do it? How did he make the leap from general knowledge, which will tell you, for example, that any vase, even if it's done nothing but sit on the same mantel for one hundred years, will still show signs of wear on the base. He has however mastered specific details that can make all the difference in identifying a piece, such as knowing that a vase you pick up is really Tiffany, even though it's not marked, because the Tiffany studios often used paper labels.

He says he's acquired most of his expertise from books, and has a library of hundreds of volumes, all related to the antiques world. "It's really the only thing I actually collect," he adds.

Books are his primary source and he buys them everywhere. However, he says he rarely spends much time in local libraries, because their collections of antiques books are outdated and limited. Surprisingly, he says that in his travels around the United States he's checked dozens and dozens of libraries, and found them all to have meager collections of books on antiques. Bookstores are apparently just the opposite. Most, he says, even in small towns and rural areas, have a remarkably sophisticated range of price guides and general information books about collectibles and antiques.

An equally important source of information is magazines. There are dozens of general interest and specific interest magazines out there, published to help you learn more about almost any topic you can imagine. If you get a chance to look at any one of the British magazines on antiques, grab it. These magazines, although expensive and hard to come by, are light years ahead of those published in this country. You can sometimes find them in bookstores with an extensive magazine section.

My dealer friend spends a lot of time exploring museums and historic restorations like Williamsburg, but says it's important, especially for newcomers to the antiques world, not to try to learn everything at once. "Pick one area or subject that really interests you," he suggests, "and find out everything you can about it, from museums, from books, price guides, talking with dealers at shows or in shops. Really study, make it a crash course and when you feel you've learned enough, go on to something else."

He also thinks it's most practical to concentrate on objects in the antiques world that you can reasonably expect to encounter. So, unless you just can't help yourself, try not to spend a whole lot of time studying esoteric areas such as medieval Japanese armor, because chances are pretty slim that you're going to run into any at a yard sale or auction.

Although, just to show you how quirky the antiques world can be, while you won't find medieval armor (all those elaborate samurai suits of armor were ceremonial anyway, and mostly made in the nineteenth century to impress people like Queen Victoria) you might actually find a fifteenth-century Japanese samurai sword in someone's front yard on a Saturday. That's because some of the most priceless swords in Japan, preserved for centuries in shrines, were picked up as souvenirs after World War II ended and were brought back to the United States. Many are still floating around out there, so if you have anything that Great Uncle Harry brought back from the war, don't do anything with it until you first have it appraised by an expert.

At the same time, my friend says, you don't want to narrow your focus too much. He sees people all the time at shows or yard sales who are hot on the trail of something truly arcane or specific, like those sterling silver posy holders women used in Victorian times to hold their tussy mussies, or little bouquets. They're so engrossed in hunting for posy holders that they overlook a lot of other fascinating things out there.

When you're out hunting, he says, look closely at what you see. Really check it out. He adds, "You'd be surprised at the number of people who barely pay attention, even when what they're going to buy is very expensive. I can't tell you the number of people who come into my shop and pick up something very valuable, decide to buy it, and say, "Can you read this price tag to me, I left my glasses in the car!"

He went on to tell me that learning the value of an unusual item can be an extremely frustrating and lengthy process, even for someone as experienced as he is:

"A while ago I bought a piece of pottery," he says, "that I knew was really good, but I had no idea what it was. Couldn't find it in any books, and nobody else here knew either. So I took it into New York City to some dealers there, and the responses I got were pretty awful. Some of them were downright rude. I think that most of them didn't know what it was either and didn't want to admit it to me, or they thought that since I'd said up front that I didn't know what it was exactly, they could get me to sell it cheap.

"And you know what, I still don't know exactly what it is, although I have a general idea it's American, and probably early twentieth century. The only progress I've made is now I have two pieces of it. I bought another last year. I'm keeping them both and sooner or later I'll find out who made them."

Collectors' clubs can be fruitful sources of information and entertainment as well. If you're interested in graniteware, for instance, it's a lot of fun to get together with other graniteware enthusiasts once in a while, and you'll probably learn as much from the group as you have from the books and articles you've been reading on your own.

Many clubs do a lot more than just providing a framework for an occasional meeting. They organize auctions or shows, let you know about other auctions and shows you might want to attend, publish newspapers and newsletters, make videos, and serve as a clearinghouse for all kinds of information about other people who share your passion.

Museums can be useful sources, too, but in general museum people tend to shy away from offering their invaluable expertise to the public. That's the result, in part, of specific policies in most museums that expressly forbid staffers from offering any evaluation of a particular item. However, what a museum can do for you is tell you where to find the ranking expert in the particular field that interests you.

So, don't call or write to the museum and say, "My grandmother left me this chair and I'd like to know what it's worth." You will get a polite rebuff.

If you only want to find out the value of one or two things, without doing a major research project, your best course of action is to wait for one of the appraisal days that are offered by many auction houses.

Butterfield & Butterfield, the California auction house that is the West Coast equivalent of Christie's and Sotheby's in New York, schedules regular walk-in days twice every month, when people can bring in anything they'd like to be evaluated and consult the appropriate expert without having to pay a fee.

The firm also makes annual "sweeps" of the United States, traveling to dozens of cities every year as part of its policy of actively looking for auction items. The appraisals are free, unless the event is sponsored by a local charity, in which case there may be a nominal fee of $5 or $10 which is donated to the charity.

Sometimes, truly astonishing things do turn up. Recently, a Butterfield & Butterfield appraiser was asked, during a taping of the "Antiques Roadshow" produced by PBS, to evaluate an old helmet that had been kept in a Philadelphia attic for years as Halloween costume material. The helmet turned out to be a sixteenth-century *cabasset* from Milan with a value of about $250,000.

Antiques dealers, who are aware of the number of people these free or minimally priced appraisals can draw, often organize a panel of local experts to do appraisals as part of the promotion for a major antiques show. They're always well advertised; just keep an eye out for them in your local paper. If you live in a small town without access to a major paper, try to subscribe to at least one area antiques publication and get your information that way. Don't go to any appraiser who says his fee will be a percentage of the piece's value.

And, finally, check around your neighborhood and see if any of the nearby dealers are offering free evening lectures by knowledgeable collectors. These events are becoming very popular in some parts of

Things You never Thought Would Be Worth Anything . . . but Really Are

1. Levi's banners. These brightly colored canvas banners, along with other Levi's promotional materials, were given away to retail stores to help sell Levi's jeans and other products. Now the banners are worth a whole lot more than any pair of jeans—$250 and up.

2. Old cereal boxes. Like old tins, cardboard cereal boxes from the thirties, forties, and fifties are prized collectibles. They're worth more unopened than if they have been emptied. A Wheaties box, for example, from the late forties, is worth about $200.

3. Old Christmas tree lights. Most people know that glass ornaments can be valuable, but the lights that went with them used to go to the dump automatically when anyone cleaned out an attic. However, there is a huge market for Christmas memorabilia, even if it's not that old. The electric bubble lights that produced a moving bubble inside a mock candle are highly prized, as are individual screw-in light bulbs molded to look like ornaments. These bulbs sell for $45 and up. Strings of lights, $30 and up to hundreds for rare designs.

4. Plastic model airplane kits. These were popular gifts for decades and a lot of them were never opened and put together. Now, the kits fetch $20 and up if all the parts are there, even for small models.

5. Electric fans. The old fans from the thirties and on up are valuable even if they don't work. However, if you can get someone to put one back in working condition, the price can easily go into the hundreds, depending upon the design.

6. Aluminum serving pieces. Those hammered aluminum trays, bowls, pitchers, and serving pieces that figured so largely in the American lifestyle of the post-war forties and fifties are being sought by an absolutely rabid group of collectors. Unusual colors are especially valued. These trendy collectors even have their own national organization and annual show. Contact American Dream Collectibles, 5128 Schultz Bridge Road, Zionsville, Pennsylvania 18092 for more information.

7. TV show games and toys. Everybody knows that lunchboxes from the sixties and seventies are hot collectibles, but would you believe an "I Dream of Jeannie" doll selling at auction for $2,437? Or a boxed "Man from U.N.C.L.E." gun going for $1,198? Also at a recent auction, a Flying Nun board game went for just over $200. Board games, toys, and television show collectibles from the sixties are all loved by baby boomers. For more information: Toy Scouts, in Akron, Ohio, at 1-216-836-0668. Also, remember the dancing and singing raisins in the popular television commercial? Yes, very hot.

8. Skookum dolls. These odd little dolls were manufactured in Denver at just about the time—thirties, forties and fifties—that Americans were taking to the road in record numbers and buying souvenirs along the way. The little male and female dolls, the most popular size just a few inches long, were always wrapped in a fragment of Indian blanket and came with a mailing label attached so they could be tossed into a mailbox after the label was filled out. They now cost $25 and up, and the larger versions go into the thousands.

9. Single drawers. Old wooden drawers, removed from a cupboard or built-in kitchen cabinet, are starting to get some designer status. They're appearing in decorating magazine layouts, individually, as containers and they cost from $45 and up. The older, more weathered and rugged they are, the better.

10. Toilet paper. It may seem hard to believe, but old toilet paper rolls have actual cash value. According to dealer Diane Foster of Westerville, Ohio, old toilet paper rolls generally go for about $2 each, but a very collectible brand such as a 1930s to 1940s Kroger, for example, might fetch $18 to $45.

the country and the practice is bound to spread. Usually, they're held after the shop or mall closes for the day, so people who attend don't feel they have to buy anything.

I went to two out of a series of six lectures at an antiques co-op and was amazed at the amount of information the speakers were able to offer. One was a woman who collected buttons and seemed to know everything there was to know about them; the second was a collector of kerosene lamps and I've never forgotten what I learned.

Because we're talking about what things are worth here, this is a good time to remind you to have photos of all your treasures, or perhaps a videotape. Store it someplace other than your home. If you lose anything, you may have trouble with your insurance company unless you can actually prove you owned it. The IRS can be even more skeptical. If your collection includes things that are very valuable, your insurer may ask you to get a written appraisal from an expert. Sometimes they'll accept your friendly local neighborhood antique dealer's appraisal, or they may ask you to hire a certified appraiser. Put any appraisal, even if it's just the comments of a show appraisal panel, in the same place where you keep your photos or videotape. (For more about appraisals, see Chapter Fifteen).

CHAPTER FOURTEEN

MOUNTAIN WEST REGION

South Dakota, North Dakota, Wyoming,
Montana, Idaho

SOUTH DAKOTA

Boyd's Antiques

This is another classic—barns in the middle of nowhere filled with stacks and stacks of wonderful stuff.

Meet Vaughn Boyd, who with his wife, Sandy,
started an antiques business seven years ago that has
now expanded to fill two huge barns and six acres.

Boyd actually had retired when he bought the
property on the highway halfway between Mount
Rushmore and Crazy Horse. Now, he says ruefully,
he's working harder than ever. He says more than
half of his merchandise is indoors, while the rest is
sprinkled around outside and includes everything
from old windmill parts to ox yokes, wooden wheels,

and horse collars. He has a gigantic collection (indoors) of old tin advertising signs—hundreds of them!

He also has western memorabilia—chaps, spurs, ropes, halters, those fairly revolting bleached cow skulls with horns—as well as fire memorabilia and Coca Cola collectibles.

There is also an outdoor display of pedal cars, those children's toy cars whose value has gone up into the thousands over the past few years, but they are Boyd's personal treasures and not for sale.

The shop is open only from May 1 to October 1 because a South Dakota winter is nothing to fool around with. He's usually open seven days a week, but call first, he says, to make sure.

TO GET THERE: Boyd's is located one-half mile north of Crazy Horse, at the intersection of US Route 16 and US 385.

FOR MORE INFORMATION: Write to Boyd's Antiques, Route 2, Custer, So. Dakota, 57730, or telephone 1-603-673-5503

NORTH DAKOTA

Wood Antiques

Bismarck is North Dakota's state capital and the city in this state in which you are most likely to find interesting antiques. Wood Antiques is just one of a number of stores clustered in downtown Bismarck, and it has a lot of interesting furniture as well as other smaller items. Some comes from Canada, a choice picking spot for dealers here. This store specializes in quartersawn oak furniture as well as other period furniture pieces including primitives. The showing space is 6,000 square feet, a lot for this city.

TO GET THERE: Bismarck is located in the center of the state; Interstate 94 will take you into the center of the city.

FOR MORE INFORMATION: Write Wood Antiques at 1514 East Thayer Avenue, Bismarck, ND 58501. The Bismarck-Mandam Convention and Visitors' Bureau will supply a map of area antiques shops and malls. Write to P.O. Box 2274 Bismarck, ND 58502

ADDENDUM: Mandam, Bismarck's sister city across the river, also has a weekend flea market in the Civic Center with fifty or sixty vendors. There are also a few antiques shops in Mandam. They're listed on the visitor's map.

WYOMING

Cody Cowboy Antique & Collectible Show & Auction

This is probably a good place to talk about western collectibles and antiques. Interestingly, although the national enthusiasm for decorating in a western mode has faded, prices for really good western collectibles are still soaring.

Bill Mackin, a collector and author of a western collectibles price guide, is extremely knowledgeable about this part of the antiques world and he says everything has gotten to be "astronomical."

"A pair of spurs that I might have paid $50 for a couple of years ago is selling for thousands, now," he says.

(Bill has donated his own collection of guns, spurs, and that sort of thing to the Armory Museum on Yampa Avenue in Craig, Colorado, the small northern town in which he lives. The museum is definitely worth a stop, as is the small antiques co-op next door called Treasures, in which Bill sells cowboy and Indian things in a back room.)

Probably the single most desirable category in western collecting, though, is not guns and spurs but furniture made by Thomas Molesworth. Not as recognizable in the East as it is in the West, Molesworth's rustic designs are so distinctive that once you've seen them, you'll know them forever. Pieces sell for thousands and thousands and they are indeed the western equivalent of the chest of gold if you find a piece.

Watch out, though, if you're after western memorabilia, for those deputy sheriff's badges, Texas ranger badges or marshall stars. The real thing is very rare; most of those you see, even at auctions, are reproductions and should sell for around $50. Also very hot: those great old cowboy hats, circa 1930, with the huge brims and high crowns.

Serious western collectors say there are only two really significant auction and show events in this country every year. One is the annual Cody show in the Cody Auditorium, and the other is in Mesa, Arizona (see Chapter Sixteen).

The Cody show and auction, now in its eighth year, brings in buyers not just from all parts of this country, but from around the world. This year, show organizer Brian Lebel has had requests for travel information and catalogs from everywhere in Europe and from Africa and Asia as well.

The show routine is the same every year. The auction is held on a Thursday, starting in the morning. The show itself, with about one hundred dealers, follows beginning Friday afternoon and runs through Sunday. The auction is free, although there is a $15 charge for an advance catalog (includes postage and a realized price list sent out after the auction is over).

Entrance fee to the show is $3; early buyers pay $30 for entrance Friday morning.

TO GET THERE: Cody is directly east of Yellowstone National Park on US Route 14. The Auditorium is located at 1240 Beck Ave.

FOR MORE INFORMATION: Write to Julia Cape, Show

Manager, P.O. Box 655, Cody, WY, 82414, or telephone 1-800-227-8483.

Rubber Snake Ranch

Antiques shops are a relatively new addition to Wyoming's cultural landscape and as a result there are only a few in the state. Indigenous antiques are virtually nonexistent; those who settled in Wyoming a long time ago often walked there or came out West on covered wagons and didn't bring a lot of unnecessary frills with them. That means, with the exception of western collectibles like branding irons, and Native American artifacts, there won't be too many breathtaking discoveries.

For a lot of Wyoming residents, antiquing means going out in the desert with a metal detector and walking along the Overland Trail and Oregon Trail routes. These routes are fairly well marked, and people say they still find treasures discarded by overloaded pioneers. The dry air and limited amount of rain keep them in good condition even though they're outdoors.

But there are exceptions to this commercial dearth of interesting western memorabilia at Bill Schenck's Rubber Snake Ranch in Moran, Wyoming, a mini-hamlet near trendy Jackson Hole.

Schenck is an artist who paints whimsical contemporary western works. He's also a collector with an eye for a bargain, and that talent has turned him into a dealer. He specializes in prehistoric Native American pottery from all over the West, but also sells fine collectibles and furniture. He says his prices are a lot lower than the shops in Jackson because he's operating out of his home and doesn't have to pay rent on a store.

Because Schenck has great taste (the log cabin he restored and decorated for nickels and dimes got a rave review in *Architectural Digest,* no small feat even for a multimillionaire), his shop is a quick cram course in what's good, great, or not so great in the world of western antiques.

Sensibly, he's only at his ranch during the warm-weather months. In November he heads back to Phoenix, Arizona, and doesn't return to the Wyoming mountains until spring. If you want to catch up with him, write or call first.

TO GET THERE: Moran is just a few miles north of Jackson on Highway 191.

FOR MORE INFORMATION: Write P.O. Box 47, Moran, WY, 83013, or telephone 1-307-543-2302 (summer); 5726 East Forest St., Apache Junction, AZ, 85220, 1-602-982-0086 (winter).

MONTANA

Broadway in Butte

Butte, Montana, is an interesting resource, local dealers say, because the town was originally a major mining center. A lot of money flowed through this western city and as a result many of its residents were able to buy beautiful things. The antiques district in Butte is located along Broadway, with perhaps a dozen stores now operating within a few blocks of each other. For information and a map, check with Antiques on Broadway, 45 Broadway, telephone 1-406-782-3207.

Depot Antiques Mall

This Billings mall is located in a picturesque old train depot. Just opened last year, it is the culmination of a dream for schoolteacher Bob Hawke, who's been pursuing a second career in antiques for years. The depot has 20,000 square feet of selling space and thirty dealers, a lot for this location, and specializes in primitives and western memorabilia along with glassware, pottery (especially Red Wing) and furniture.

TO GET THERE: The mall is located at 2223 Montana Ave., Billings, MT, 59101.
FOR MORE INFORMATION: Telephone 1-406-245-5955.

IDAHO

Coeur d'Alene Antiques Mall

This is the largest mall in Idaho and it has now expanded to two locations with a dealer population of 125.

Mall owner Jan Shubert, who was the first person in the state to develop antiques malls, now operates her two locations seven days a week, except for Thanksgiving and Christmas. The malls carry a lot of western collectible memorabilia as well as Native American items and railroad collectibles, along with fine antiques and pottery and china.

TO GET THERE: Coeur d'Alene is in northern Idaho, 30 miles east of Spokane, Washington. Interstate 90 goes directly through it.

FOR MORE INFORMATION: The two mall locations are at: W. 408 Haycroft, and No. 3650 Government Way, Coeur d'Alene, Idaho 83814, or telephone 1-208-667-0246.

ADDENDUM: Most of the Idaho dealers buy at local rural auctions, which are conducted year-round in the state. They also go across the border to Spokane, Washington which has a number of good dealer resources. There are some antiques shops in Boise, Idaho, and in Idaho Falls, Idaho, which is located just over the mountain from trendy Jackson Hole, Wyoming.

CHAPTER FIFTEEN

CASHING IN ON YOUR COLLECTION

Inevitably, there's going to be a time when you want to sell off some of your treasures. It doesn't really matter whether you're running out of room or running out of money, your choices of how to go about getting a fair price for the things you want to sell are essentially the same, with one important exception.

If you can make time your ally instead of an enemy, you will almost always be able to realize a better profit on what you sell. If you can't afford to wait, or have an estate you need to settle quickly, it can be more difficult to realize the best possible price.

Disposing of antiques, unlike selling off stocks and bonds, is not a neat, orderly process that offers the same predictable rate of return as do other investments. Be prepared, before you even begin the process of "deaccessioning" as the museums like to call it, to accept the fact that some of your treasures may have increased in value, but others might actually be worth less than what you paid for them.

I once met a woman who told me she used the little spare cash she was able to set aside each week to buy small collectibles, mostly at yard sales. She didn't display them; instead, she packed them carefully in boxes and says she's not even going to look at them for another ten years. By that time, her daughter will be ready for college and she sees her collectibles as an investment that will return enough cash to help with her daughter's tuition.

It will be interesting to see how that turns out, but I wouldn't count on it. Antiques, like everything else, seem to have their fifteen minutes of fame and then fade.

One day when I was out West, a young man staggered in the door of my shop, struggling under the weight of a huge wooden box full of glass insulators. He was carrying them as though he had crown jewels in that box and told me he'd stumbled across this mother lode out in one of the remote western deserts. When I broke the news to him that insulators don't sell anymore unless they are extremely rare varieties, and even then it's a long wait, he was so disappointed he looked as though he was having one of those coal-in-your-stocking Christmas mornings.

Now, there are still a few insulator collectors out there. They have clubs, an annual convention in

Texas, and even a few price guides. But the days when insulator collecting was a huge hobby are long gone.

Other larger categories in collecting have suffered similar fates. A few years ago, Oprah Winfrey spent a quarter of a million dollars at one auction alone, buying up Shaker furniture. Shaker was really hot, then—Barbra Streisand was collecting it, too—and pieces that had sold for a few hundred just a year or so earlier were going for thousands. Then, just as abruptly, the Shaker market collapsed, in part because a lot of very unsaintly Shaker of dubious origin came on the market and was incorrectly attributed to the small religious sect.

Duck decoys have dropped in price, too. The end came for speculators in that game during one particularly disastrous auction, when prices crashed and burned. They've never really recovered.

And how about baseball cards? All sports cards, actually, and a lot of sports memorabilia as well. Prices soared for a while, but a lot of people who were putting investment money into cards because the profit was so spectacular learned, to their sorrow, how fleeting financial fame can be.

Of course, you may wonder how that jibes with the fact that a Honus Wagner card, which is essentially the Holy Grail of all baseball cards, just sold at auction for $580,000.

Any really good antique is going to hold its value. The top of the line in any area, whether it's Shaker or duck decoys, is still going to sell for a lot of money, usually more than its previous owner paid. But anything that's not quite the cream of the crop is going to be more vulnerable to the vagaries of the marketplace.

Western memorabilia, for example, is not as fashionable as it used to be. I've been watching the lower end of the western collectibles field start to show up at yard sales, always a good indicator that a trend has passed. However, the very best western antiques and collectibles, the real top-of-the-line stuff, is selling for astronomical prices to dedicated collectors. They may not be as trendy a group as they used to be, but they're willing to pay almost anything for a desirable piece of pottery or pair of spurs.

Now that you know that you have to be prepared for both good-news and bad-news responses to your antiques' value, how do you actually sell them?

Here's another piece of good news. A group of things almost always is more valuable than a single item or a pair. A few years ago I saw a collection of child-sized Indian moccasins. There were at least twenty pairs, some great, some so-so, and all mounted in a circle on a piece of green painted plywood. The final effect was fantastic and the asking price for the collection was $50,000. One of those pairs of moccasins would have sold for $350 to $1,000, depending upon age and the quality of workmanship.

This is a good place to mention that if anything

in your collection is cracked, dinged, chipped, broken, or repaired, no matter how artfully, or if it has replacement parts, upholstery, rungs, or wiring, or if it has been repainted or stripped, the value is almost always going to be substantially less than it is for something in pristine condition.

There are very few exceptions. But, should you find a discolored, ripped, and torn original copy of the Declaration of Independence, it wouldn't matter how damaged it might be if it were authentic. Condition is still relative to rarity.

Remember the Milwaukee couple who found a real Van Gogh in their attic? It was not a very good Van Gogh, and it was in poor condition, but because it was a real Van Gogh, it still commanded a six-figure price at auction.

But these are the exceptions that prove the rule. You can't expect to get much more than a fraction of its value for something that's been damaged. For example, you've inherited Great Aunt Emma's Haviland china dinner set with the painted violets and gold rim. It's almost all there, but a couple of cups are missing, the lid for the teapot has a little crack, and so does a platter. Does this minor damage really affect value? You bet it does. In fact, you can automatically deduct a lot of points for any kind of china set that's not complete. For bargain hunters, this is a good thing to know because it makes incomplete sets very inexpensive. Then, if you have the time and patience (I don't) you can comb through antiques shops and all those replacement china ads in the backs of magazines to make up the complete set.

Now, here's my big rule when you're trying to sell things. Never, ever let a dealer into your house. Well, there may be the exception here, too, if you have a good friend who's a dealer and trustworthy enough to give you a fair and honest appraisal of the things you want to sell. But don't count on it.

The economics of the antiques business dictate that dealers who want to survive have to be able to buy low and sell high. When you invite a dealer in to look over your finds and give you a price for them, you are usually a sitting duck.

From the dealer's point of view, going to someone's home to give a price estimate is often a waste of time. A lot of people think they can get a free appraisal by calling in a dealer, announcing they have lots to sell, and asking the dealer what each piece of furniture or glassware might bring. Soon it becomes apparent that the person really doesn't intend to sell anything.

So what happens most of the time is a sort of Abbot and Costello routine. The purported seller, pointing to a desk in the living room, says, "How much is this worth?"

The dealer replies, "How much do you want for it?" And this kind of cagey game can go on and on until one of the parties realizes they're getting nowhere and quits.

Unscrupulous dealers sometimes try to bully people into selling their treasures for very little. They stalk through a house, muttering that everything's junk, and then as they're leaving, casually offer you $50 for the secretary in the corner that's worth at least a thousand.

If you do want a dealer to come in and make an offer, try to do a little advance research, even if it's just glancing through a few books, so you have a general idea of value.

What I used to do, when people asked me to take a look at things they wanted to sell, was tell them exactly what I would sell it for, and then explain how much I could pay, taking into consideration condition, repairs needed, and desirability. That way, when they came into my shop, they wouldn't gasp in surprise at the retail price of the items they'd sold to me.

My offer was usually anywhere from twenty to fifty percent of what my selling price was going to be, fair enough if you take the dealer's side for a moment and realize the dealer has to stand the cost of rent, utilities, advertising, and all the rest of the expenses of operating a retail business, then add them to the base price of the item just to be able to break even without making a profit.

Unfortunately, unscrupulous dealers aren't content with making a reasonable profit; they want the biggest markup they can get, and if that requires a little deception, they'll do it. Fortunately, you now may have legal recourse if a dealer deliberately undervalues your antiques.

There's a very interesting case that has been the subject of several *Maine Antique Digest* stories. It all began with an Indian blanket. The owner had asked a dealer with whom he was friendly to tell him what the blanket was worth. The dealer suggested a price range and then offered to buy the blanket himself. The seller, trusting the appraisal, agreed and only much later learned that the dealer had in turn sold the very rare chief's blanket for thousands and thousands of dollars. The seller sued and the case is still going on. The decision should be a landmark.

If you are trying to settle an estate or have an extensive collection yourself, you may want to hire a professional appraiser. It's going to cost you; appraisals don't come cheap, which is why people are always trying to get dealers to do theirs for nothing. But you will have a reasonable idea of value against which to negotiate with dealers or auctioneers. Make sure the appraiser you hire is credentialed and check references.

If you think that you have discovered a major find, a true treasure that is worth a lot of money, you can ask one of the major auction houses to evaluate it for you. Have a few good quality photographs taken that show as much detail as possible, then call the auction house and find out the name of the person who specializes in this area of interest. Don't bother trying to discuss the virtues of the piece on the telephone; it's not worth their time or yours until they actually see the photos.

When you send them in to the auction house, include as many details as you can about the piece— where it came from, how long it's been in the possession of your family, etc. This is the provenance, the record of its past, and it may be very important. Provenance, by the way, has to be anchored in verifiable fact and written records; word of mouth isn't good enough.

Once I had a woman come into my shop and ask me how much I thought she could get for a brandy decanter that had belonged to Napoleon. The bottle was the right age, but there was nothing to link it to Napoleon other than family legend. So the association with a famous world leader didn't affect the price at all because it couldn't be proved.

If the auction house wants to know where you found your particular treasure if it's not a family heirloom, tell them the truth, but you don't have to be specific. You can always say "at a recent auction" or "from a private sale" without revealing the amount you paid. They'll probably try to find that out, too, but you're under no obligation to provide that kind of information. Simply tell them, "I'd rather not say."

It's my personal opinion that some of the major houses like to get a provenance from the seller as well as for the piece. If I'm Nancy Nobody I'm not going to get ecumenical treatment and that is, I suppose, human nature.

What this translates into in practical terms is: if you decide to send photos to one of the major auction houses, don't write the accompanying letter in crayon. Spring for some upscale stationery and if you have a business letterhead and dealer's resale number, so much the better.

It's usually not a good idea to consign to an auction house unless you have a lot of things to sell. For a single item, it's worth it only if there is going to be a lot of room between what you paid for it and what you expect to get out of it. In the posh auction houses, you have to pay a seller's premium, plus a fee for a catalog listing, plus an additional fee if that listing is going to be accompanied by an illustration or photo. By the time you get through with all the charges, all your profit may go into fees.

Always, always, always set a reserve. The better auction houses will remind you, sometimes, to do so. The lesser ones, or more casual and rural auctioneers, may not. But unless you want to see your consigned items sell for almost nothing, make sure you have set a realistic reserve well in advance of the auction date.

If the auction house tells you they never put reserves on their sale items, look for another auctioneer, no matter how much they insist they'll sell your things for a good price. It's simply not worth the risk, and I've never heard of anyone who's sold through an auction with no reserve and been happy with the results.

The reserve is the lowest price you'll accept in the sale. Keep in mind, when you're figuring out what your reserve ought to be, that fees have to be deducted before you'll see any real profit.

However, you have to recognize that the reserve has got to be at the lower end of the value spectrum. Here's how it works. If you have a pair of blue Heisey glass horse bookends that are worth, according to price guides, $185, you can't consider that amount the reserve. It will have to be a little less, depending upon how badly you want to sell the bookends. You already know that dealers won't pay more than fifty percent of the price they expect to get, so let's say the top a dealer would pay is $90. That's a fair reserve, or you could go a little higher, hoping a collector is willing to outbid the dealers in the room, and set your reserve at $125. Out of that amount, of course, you have to pay the auction house a percentage.

Especially on larger, more valuable items, the auction house probably will tell you what kind of reserve to put in place. It's up to you to figure out if that price estimate is an acceptable bottom line before you make a commitment to the sale.

Make sure you have all the auction terms and fees, as well as any reserves, in writing, even if the auctioneer is your brother-in-law. Once I consigned a lot of antiques to an auctioneer I trusted. I wasn't able to attend the auction, and because I hadn't bothered to put reserves on everything I lost out badly. It was and still is a painful lesson.

If you feel, even after you've consulted one of the major auction houses, that the real value of your piece hasn't been recognized, try another auction house, or wait six months or so and then try to find out what it's worth again.

Auction houses, even very reputable and prominent ones, do occasionally make mistakes. There is a lawsuit underway now in England brought by a man who took an old painting out of the attic to his local auctioneer. It was sold at auction for a few thousand dollars because the auctioneer said it was "not quite right." Not quite right is Britishese for phony as a three-dollar bill, and the seller was quite happy with the few thousand dollars he received for this copy of an old master until the dealer who'd bought it sold it again in London a few months later. There it was considered more than just a little right because it went for six figures.

If you're willing to wait, you can probably get a better price by consigning your things to an antiques dealer with an established shop. Before you do, make sure you have all the provisions of your consignment agreement in writing. Usually, dealers who accept consignments will ask for a fifty-fifty split and will have a time limit. After sixty days or so, they either own the merchandise outright unless you remove it, or can sell at dramatically lower prices.

Make sure you're clear about the time factor. It's usually the consignor's responsibility to pick up the merchandise if it doesn't sell.

You can probably realize the most profit on a sale by offering your things to someone who is a collector. For example, even though the antique brandy decanter that belonged to Napoleon had no provenance, it might have been of interest to someone in the Napoleon Society, a group of admirers of the French emperor who meet regularly, have a newsletter and an annual convention accompanied by an antiques show and auction.

Recently, I bought a piece of unusually colorful graniteware. If I decide I want to sell it, I'll contact the National Graniteware Society in Cedar Rapids, Iowa. The organization also sponsors an annual convention and auction/show.

If you're looking for a specific type of collector, read the antiques trade papers carefully. Many add to their collections by soliciting through ads. You can also advertise yourself; in most of the trade publications, ads are very inexpensive.

Also look for announcements about upcoming shows featuring similar items and contact dealers who will be exhibiting in them.

Some Very Interesting Prices

- A tramp art wall box inlaid with mahogany—$1,045 at an auction in Maine.
- Green swirl graniteware cream can—$2,500 at the annual graniteware collectors' auction in Springfield, Illinois.
- A one-quart glass flask in "Baltimore Glass Works" and Anchor/Sheaf of Grain patterns from 1860–1870 in a clear and brilliant blue—$16,500 at a bottle collectors' auction in Massachusetts.
- Fine, extremely well-detailed two-story doll house almost four feet wide with interior wallpaper—$5,500 at the annual Manchester, New Hampshire antiques show.
- An unsigned mission oak Morris chair with worn leather upholstery—$2,420 at a Maine auction.
- Dog portrait, circa 1919 by British artist Monica Gray—$2,750 at an auction conducted by Pettigrew's in Colorado Springs, Colorado.
- A long, tall cut-glass vase, signed by Hawkes and made in 1902, 48" high—$24,500 from a Texas dealer showing in Washington D.C.
- Leather-bound, woven rattan fishing creel in excellent condition—$7,480, a new creel record, at an auction in Boxborough, Massachusetts.
- Fiesta mixing bowl lid, six #3, with a hard-to-find lid with a chip—$412.50 at a special auction of Fiesta dinnerware and serving pieces in Ft. Wayne, Indiana.
- Alphabet Man, a rare metal educational toy made in the late-nineteenth century, missing a lever with a badly paint-flaked face—$23,575 at Skinner's Auction House in Bolton, Massachusetts.
- Miniature cast-iron stove from the early-twentieth century, 18" long and 22" high—$550 in a Vermont antique mall.

CHAPTER SIXTEEN

WESTERN REGION

Colorado, Utah, Nevada,
Arizona, New Mexico, Texas

COLORADO

Stage Stop Antique Mall

This mall on the outskirts of Denver has done such good business that it's doubled its selling space during the past year, expanding to fill another store in the building. Now there are more than one hundred dealers in this very western mall. Most are on the ground floor, although at the left and in the back of the building are small stairways leading up to a partial second floor where the best furniture bargains will be found. Because Denver's history encompasses gold rushes, silver mining, cattle wars, and oil wells, there are lots of treasures of all kinds to be found—everything from elaborate Victorian oil paintings to old pack saddles and beaded vests. The mall is frequented by dealers who travel hundreds of miles to buy here. The beginning of the week always seems to be the best time for bargains.

However, watch out for the reproduction prints in old frames: they're extremely good copies of famous nineteenth- and twentieth-century prints, which means they might not always be readily recognizable as new.

TO GET THERE: Interstate 70, which runs east-west through Denver; take Exit 269, then south on Wadsworth Blvd. to 44th Avenue and turn left. The mall is just behind a Perkins restaurant on the right side of 44th Ave.

FOR MORE INFORMATION: Write Stage Stop Antique Mall, 7340 W. 44th Ave. Wheat Ridge, Colorado, or telephone 1-303-423-3630

ADDENDUM: Denver's antiques district, a row of several dozen shops and malls along both sides of the street, runs along South Broadway in downtown Denver.

You can also find good buys at a row of flea markets that are located north of Denver, near the college town of Fort Collins, which is about ninety miles from the city. Take US Route 287 North; the malls are right on the road on the north side of the town.

West Antiques

Terry and Nancy West started their antiques shop fifteen years ago in two small rooms with less than

1,000 square feet of selling space. Now they've expanded to take over an entire city block, 13,000 square feet of selling space, with their collection of low-priced antique furniture.

This is one of the places you hear about from a friend. Until very recently, the Wests did almost no advertising because they didn't have to. Terry says their volume is so high that the store sells in a week what the average antiques shop would sell in a year. Merchandise comes in by the truckload at least two or three times a week, and it's all refinished or refurbished in an on-premises workshop so that it's all ready to sell or use. Prices are incredible, usually about half the normal retail.

West's also supplements the furniture with some antique decorative accessories and some small reproduction items. There's also a decorating service operated in conjunction with the shop, and West's has just created a computer request service so that buyers can be notified when the particular item they want arrives in a new shipment. Voted the best antiques shop in Colorado by *Westword,* a Denver magazine. Open seven days, 10 to 7, except Sundays, 12 to 5.

TO GET THERE: West is in Lafayette, Colorado, seven miles east of Boulder and seven miles west of Interstate 25, the primary north-south artery in the state.

FOR MORE INFORMATION: Write to 401/409 So. Public Rd, Lafayette, Colorado or telephone, 1-303-666-7200.

UTAH

Salt Lake City Salt Palace

James Reese, who is the publisher of *New Century Collector,* an antiques trade newspaper in Utah, also organizes shows; his fall and spring shows at the Salt Lake City Salt Palace are the top dealer attractions in the state every year.

(Walter Larsen, another show promoter in the city, also does a spring and a fall show at the Expo Mart behind the Salt Palace.)

Reese says the local dealers like to hunt for antiques at the Redwood Swap Meet on Redwood Road in Salt Lake. The Swap Meet is held every week on Saturdays and Sundays.

He also says that in addition to shops in Salt Lake's antiques district, most of them clustered in a downtown area along South 300 Street and State Street, Provo, Utah, notable for Robert Redford's Sundance resort, and Ogden, Utah, also have begun to establish interesting multidealer antiques districts.

FOR MORE INFORMATION: Write to James Reese at the *New Century Collector,* P.O. Box 510432, Salt Lake City, UT, 84151, or telephone 1-810-532-3401

NEVADA

Las Vegas Malls

Something very interesting has been happening in Las Vegas. Maybe it's all those buildings that seem to be coming down and going up; maybe it's a reflection of the growing national interest in antiques; maybe it's the result of the population explosion in the city itself. Whatever the reason, Las Vegas is going berserk for antiques. In the last two-and-a-half years, more than one hundred shops have opened in one section of the city, creating an entire antiques district.

You'd expect to find gambling memorabilia in Vegas and there's plenty of it in these stores. Less predictably, the million or so residents of the city are entranced by nineteen-fifties furniture and memorabilia, and there's lots of it to find here because the dealers say it sells so well.

There is also a good selection of country furniture, glassware, jewelry, and even some very expensive European pieces.

The reason all this is happening, according to Buddy Lampkin, the manager of the Red Rooster Mall, is "because we're a 'come-in' town. Everybody's comin' here from somewhere else."

Lampkin, like his midwestern peer, John Kruesel, loves lighting fixtures and lamps and has been dealing in them for more than twenty-five years. He has an impressive roster of dealer customers who come to him from all the surrounding states. He sells through a booth in the mall, but estimates only about ten percent of his sales go through the store. The rest of his stock is located at his home, and he says that if you come to the Red Rooster and ask him, you'll be able to get his private telephone number and address. He brings lighting material in from all over the Midwest, he says, making three or four big buying trips each year.

The rest of the sixty dealers in the Red Rooster have all kinds of other antiques in the 25,000 square foot mall. A Las Vegas newspaper poll rated this mall the most enjoyable place to shop for antiques in the city, and one of the participating dealers cheerfully describes the rambling warren of room-style booths as "complete chaos." Open seven days.

TO GET THERE: The Red Rooster is located at the southeastern corner of Charleston and Interstate 15, about a half mile from the Las Vegas strip. Don't walk it; take a cab because the neighborhood's not that great.

FOR MORE INFORMATION: Write to Red Rooster at 1109 Western Ave., Las Vegas, NV, 89102, or telephone 1-702-382-5253.

Another interesting antiques place to check out is a new small strip mall of a half-dozen antiques shops on Tropicana dominated by the Antique Sampler, a

40,000 square foot store with more upscale merchandise, including estate jewelry. The Sampler also has a tea room and patio cafe. Open seven days.

TO GET THERE: This small mall is located about three miles from the Vegas strip. Take a cab.

FOR MORE INFORMATION: Write Joy Hermias, Manager, the Antique Sampler, at 6115 West Tropicana, or telephone 1-702-368-1170.

The third Vegas mall of interest is the Gypsy Caravan, a flamboyant shop that features casino memorabilia, movie props, and other antiques in one huge 25,000 square foot room. Owner Veronica Holmes, who used to be based in Houston, says that her pickers from all over the West are bringing her new merchandise every week.

TO GET THERE: The store is in the antique district at 624 So. Maryland Parkway at the corner of Charleston.

FOR MORE INFORMATION: Telephone 1-702-384-1870

ARIZONA

Mesa Cowboy Antiques Show and Auction

This annual January event is considered by collectors to be one of the two most important show and auction events held in this country for western dealers and collectors. The other is held in the summer in Cody, Wyoming, (see Page 195).

More than 160 dealers, all of them specializing in top quality, high-end western memorabilia, show at the Centennial Hall in Mesa during the weekend of the third week in January every year.

This show, like the Cody event, attracts customers from all over the world. The show itself is held on Saturday and Sunday. There is an early admission fee of $25 to get in on Friday, during dealer set-up. The auction preview, also on Saturday, is free. The auction itself is always held on Saturday evening.

Pre-auction catalogs, and travel and room discount information is available in December.

TO GET THERE: Mesa itself is a bedroom community close to both Scottsdale, Arizona, and Phoenix, Arizona. The Centennial Hall is located at 201 Center Street, about twenty minutes from the Phoenix Airport and adjacent to the Sheraton Hotel.

FOR MORE INFORMATION: Write to: Linda Kohn, 9929 Venice Boulevard, Los Angeles, CA, 90034, or telephone 1-310-202-9010.

Phoenix Fairgrounds Antiques Market

With a couple of exceptions in the dates, there is a monthly antiques and collectibles show at the Phoenix Fairgrounds that attracts from two hundred to six hundred dealers each time, depending upon the season. More dealers always appear during the winter months, when Arizona fills up with seasonal residents and visitors, and the dealers themselves like to get away from cold temperatures in the north. Some dealers come from as far away as the East Coast and many are from the Midwest.

The show is held on Saturday and Sunday every month, except for October. It is always on the third weekend of the month, except in December when it could conflict with Christmas. Setup is on Friday and there is a $20 early admission fee. Market admission is only $1 but there is a $4 parking fee.

TO GET THERE: State Fairgrounds, 1826 West McDowell.

FOR MORE INFORMATION: Telephone 1-601-943-1766

NEW MEXICO

Most of the western states have been growing in population during the past decade, but New Mexico has emerged as the most trendy place to live, its towns and cities replete with artists, craftsmen and -women, movie stars, and other affluent newcomers.

Antiques shops in the state, consequently, tend to cater to the new influx of wealthier residents and, especially in the larger cities, prices seem to be as high or higher than you'd expect in the most exclu-

sive stores in the East. There are not many bargains to be found, and the Native American market has become so rarefied that few people can venture into collecting in this area unless they have a lot of disposable income.

Collecting Native American antiques is controversial here because there have been intense debates about the morality of buying and selling objects that Native American tribes regard as religiously significant. This conflict reached its peak a few years ago at a New York City antiques show when the FBI arrived and confiscated a mask, which had been sold for a sum of six figures, as stolen property. Tribal elders had claimed the mask had been removed illegally from a secret religious site. The mask eventually was returned to them.

For their part, New Mexico dealers say that it's not unusual for a valuable authentic piece to be sold and resold, only to be confiscated by the authorities, and returned to the tribe from which it was removed.

The result? While the debate continues, any purchase of expensive Native American artifacts is dicey. If ever there were a time when provenance is important, it's in this aspect of the antiques market. Getting a guarantee of not only authenticity but rightful ownership is vital. Less expensive souvenir merchandise, and some modest authentic pieces— pottery, horse blankets, antique jewelry—can still be found.

The best time and place to look is in the month

of August, when thousands of people come to New Mexico for the Indian Market in Santa Fe, which is always conducted on the third weekend of August. In the week preceding the actual Market weekend, there is always a major ethnographic antiques show at the Sweeney Center, Santa Fe's convention hall.

The Indian Market is not an antiques show. It is a gathering of at least twelve hundred Native American artisans and merchants who set up and sell their wares in Santa Fe's central square, the Plaza, and the streets that surround it. However, because there are so many people who attend the Market, antiques dealers in the city and in surrounding areas always offer special promotions and discounts at this time as well.

El Collectivo Antiques Market

Santa Fe does have one small dealer mall with moderately priced merchandise, much of it cowboy kitsch and Native American. The mall has fifteen dealers and takes in a lot of consignment merchandise, which is how owner Vikki Thompson is able to acquire authentic western memorabilia. The mall does not stock any reproduction material.

TO GET THERE: El Collectivo is located in the DeVargas Center, a shopping mall at 556 No. Guadeloupe, Santa Fe, NM, 87501

FOR MORE INFORMATION: Telephone 1-505-820-7205.

ADDENDUM: The Santa Fe Convention and Tourism Bureau will be happy to send a visitor's guide, which includes information about the Indian Market. Telephone 1-800-777-2489. The Market itself is organized by the Southwest Indian Artists' Association, which will supply more detailed information. Telephone, 1-505-783-5220.

TEXAS

Round Top Roundup

In April and again in October, collectors and dealers from all over the country head for the tiny town of Round Top, midway between Houston and Austin.

More than three hundred dealers gather at this biannual event to show their best country, folk, and primitive acquisitions. Although there are a few dealers who offer some fancier antiques, the bulk of the merchandise at Round Top is good country style.

The show is spread out in three places. It started twenty-six years ago in the Rifle Association Hall, which still hosts thirty-two dealers, many regulars and some who've been with the show since it began. Another eighty or more dealers display in adjacent tents.

The organizer, Emma Lee Turley, added a second location five years ago—the New Pavilion, which has sixty dealers—and then a third, the old Carmine Dance Hall six miles away on Highway 290.

There is no early admission at Round Top, so dealers and collectors have to vie equitably at the starting time of 9:00 A.M. Friday. The show runs for three days.

TO GET THERE: West from Houston or East from Austin on US Route 290. You'll see the Carmine Dance Hall dealers first.

FOR MORE INFORMATION: Write Emma Lee Turley, P.O. Box 8221289, Houston, TX, or telephone 1-713-493-5501.

First Monday Flea Market

This is one of the top outdoor markets in the country. Every month, as many as five thousand vendors come here to sell, and a lot of them are antiques dealers. Although it's called First Monday, that's certainly a misnomer, because it's actually conducted over the weekend preceding the first Monday of the month.

In fact, the real action takes place even before the weekend begins, because dealers start to arrive and set up on Thursday evening. There's a lot of the usual barter-by-flashlight business conducted Thursday night and early Friday morning, so among the professional buyers and sellers, the weekend is over almost before it begins.

However, there is an unreserved section of the market, and vendors line up to get in here by 7:00 A.M. This western section of the market, which is close to another indoor antiques market in the Civic Center, is known locally as "the glory hole" and it's the portion of the market knowledgeable dealers check out first.

TO GET THERE: Canton is sixty miles east of Dallas and one-and-a-half miles south of Interstate 20 on Highway 19.

FOR MORE INFORMATION: Write to P.O. Box 245, Canton, TX, 75103, or telephone 1-903-567-6556.

CHAPTER SEVENTEEN

WHAT'S HOT, WHAT'S NOT

What kind of antiques offer the best return on your money right now?

Original art is still an awfully good buy. Not everyone is going to turn up a missing Van Gogh, but there are some very valuable works waiting to be discovered, many tucked away in shops and malls far from the major industrial centers.

Most often, the reason these valuable oils, pastels, acrylics, and watercolors haven't been snapped up already is their framing. A poor or outdated frame can have a horrendous effect on the work it is supposed to enhance.

For inexplicable reasons, a lot of people won't buy a painting that's been done on canvas board rather than stretched canvas. There's no good reason I've ever been able to find to support this prejudice, but it does exist.

If you can separate a painting from its frame, you will be in a much better position to assess its true value. If you can't remove the art from the frame, try to mask the frame with neutral paper, or newspaper if you have to, and you'll be able to get a better idea of what it really looks like.

Reframing, as you probably already know, can be wildly expensive. Sometimes you can fit a new acquisition into a frame you already own by having a new mat cut for it. This works very well for watercolors, prints, and some pastels. Old photographs, also very collectible and now rising astronomically in price, can benefit from new matting as well. It's harder to do with oils, because they are so much more dimensional and matting often makes an oil look a little cheesy.

The framer is not likely to smile warmly at you when you saunter in carrying an old frame and ask him or her to cut a mat to fit it, because matting is the least expensive part of a framing job. I do it anyway, occasionally, and I've also had a lot of luck with precut mats, available in craft supply stores and some photography or stationery shops.

Oils and other works on stretched canvas or canvas board require a little more work to convert into an existing frame. Most framers won't cut down an old frame for you—that's asking too much—so you have very little choice. You'll have to change the shape of the artwork itself to conform to the frame in which you plan to fit it. This is tough to do with canvas board, because you can have a hard time finding the right edges to trim and any mistake you make is irrevocable. It is possible, though, with plain stretched canvas because it's fairly easy to remove the canvas from its stretchers, the boards that hold the canvas. Replace the old stretchers with new ones that correspond to the size of the inner edges of the frame, staple the canvas in place again, and your painting will fit back into the frame as though it had been made for it.

Or, you can do what my New Hampshire friend Toy Storey does. She has built up a fantastic art collection over the years, most of it Early American and almost all acquired inexpensively. She measures each piece as she gets it and if it needs a better frame, she jots the dimensions down in a little notebook she carries everywhere because she's incredibly well-organized. What she does, and what you're supposed to do, is whip out your notebook and measuring tape any time you spot a frame you like and then consult your waiting list for a possible fit.

Of course, if you're like me, you've forgotten to bring the notebook and the tape on the day you finally do find a frame, so you eyeball it, decide it looks as though one of your pieces of art should fit into it, buy it, and then discover when you get it home that nothing you own does fit. Then the frame gets added to the dozen others you bought the same way that don't fit with anything either.

Although I would relegate them to that category called "personal taste," which usually means dubious taste, the hottest new collectible is the paint-by-number picture. I've seen them priced at $100 or more, which I have to admit leaves me open-mouthed with astonishment. But apparently, trendy people can't wait to buy them.

Another category that is beginning to build into a hot collectible is any kind of needlework. Hand-embroidered pillowcases, needlepoint throw pillows, hooked rugs, or almost anything else that's been stitched, sewn, or crocheted are beginning to go up in value, and I suspect will climb considerably higher fairly quickly.

Folk art of any kind also attracts sophisticated collectors and it's hard to go wrong buying birdhouses, doll houses, whirligigs or homemade toys, as long as you're certain they're authentic.

Almost any child's toy with any age to it has value that is bound to increase. However, condition is extremely important. One of the most influential upscale firms dealing in antique toys is named Mint and Boxed, which gives you a good clue.

Children's pedal cars are hugely popular, and restoration doesn't seem to make them lose value, although of course a pedal car that's practically new will bring a lot more than one that's been repainted and given a new set of wheels. Some of the more unusual pedal cars, such as a 1940's airplane, sell for many thousands of dollars.

Dolls, old and new, have overtaken stamps as the biggest collecting hobby in this country. There is the usual plethora of doll magazines, newspapers, price guides, clubs, contests, and conventions, and they operate almost everywhere. However, the Cabbage Patch dolls, which are listed in some of the price guides as having an automatic value of from $35 to $150 at a minimum for some of the mass-produced models, and up into the thousands for the first, custom-produced dolls, don't seem to trade very briskly to the general public the way other collectible or antique dolls do.

The mass-produced Cabbage Patch dolls should be going up in value rapidly because the firm that used to make them is now out of business and the name was sold. But that *should* is strictly theoretical because every dealer I've ever met who sells dolls has a huge box of those Cabbage Patch people stored and waiting for the day they finally become popular. They sure aren't now.

My experience with a Cabbage Patch doll is a good example of how not to buy into a presumed trend just to make money. I love antique dolls but the Cabbage Patch creatures are not way up there on my list of favorites. Then I learned from an ardent Cabbage Patch collector (some do exist) that a particular mass-produced doll, the red-headed boy, was worth at least a thousand if it could be found because so few were made.

Well, of course I kept an eye out for that red-headed boy doll from then on, and one day I found one, I paid about $50 for it, cheap, I figured for a doll that was worth a thousand. I called a Cabbage Patch expert in Florida and then found out that no, it wasn't just the red-headed boy, it was the blue-eyed, red-headed boy. The brown-eyed version, which of course is the one I'd found, wasn't worth what I paid for it.

Variations on that theme abound in the antiques world. It's wise, when you're thinking in terms of investments, to only buy what you really like. All too often if you pick up something simply because you think you've found a small-fortune-in-the-making, you'll learn that it isn't really that valuable because there's some arcane bit of knowledge you didn't have in advance.

Other important upcoming trends? Well, I've suddenly discovered that white ironstone pitchers, and to some extent any old white ironstone china, is become hugely popular. I saw, at a recent show, a very attractive booth that contained only footed cake plates and white ironstone pitchers, with a few delicate linens tossed around as background. The booth looked great and those pitchers were moving very briskly at eyebrow-raising prices of more than $150 each. The best ones were going for more than $200, and there wasn't a footed cake plate in the lot for less than $75. The pitchers didn't come with bowls, although they probably all started out that way. When I talked to the dealer who had decided to specialize in this limited field, she told me that it was easy to pick up pitchers with dings and chips or cracks. Most of these old pitchers do have them because the were in constant use along with their accompanying bowls before the advent of running water. The hard part, she said, was finding them without imperfections, and that's why the price was so high. The bowls, incidentally, don't seem to interest buyers as much.

Linens and laces are going up in price, too. They are becoming scarce even in the East, where there used to be a ready supply. Costume jewelry is a difficult field to get into now, because there are so many jewelry dealers already operating in the market. That makes it hard to buy and sell later at a better price.

You're actually better off investing in estate jewelry with gemstones or semiprecious stones set in gold, silver, or platinum. Prices are still quite modest, and most jewelry sells for a lot less than it's worth. Estate jewelry auctions are very popular in Europe, where everyone seems to know this is one area of the antiques market that's still undervalued.

Anything made from wood is going to increase in value even more than it already has. The reason? A few years ago, the federal government raised the prices it charges for lumber cut on federal land. That meant that raw wood prices increased sharply, and are continuing to go up. In turn, this means new furniture prices are beginning to soar.

When new furniture gets more expensive, people tend to hang onto their old stuff, even if they don't like it. They'd much rather get rid of Grandma's old Victorian parlor set, but they can't afford to replace it just yet, so the market slows as fewer pieces are sold. Then, as demand begins to outpace supply, prices go up.

Every dealer I've met in every part of this country tells me the same thing: good antique furniture is in increasingly short supply. If you find something you like, don't wait for a few years to buy because the price is going to be a lot more.

There's also the exception that proves the rule, and in furniture that means American Empire pieces. For years, dealers in the Northeast have been stockpiling these pieces, made from the Revolutionary War era through the mid-nineteenth century, in the expectation that the price is going to skyrocket any day now. Sadly, stubbornly, American Empire pieces stay put. They don't move rapidly out of shops and the price is not going up. It's hard to understand this because the look isn't fussy, although the pieces tend to be dark and massive. Still, people just don't buy it.

However, if you look at the Ralph Lauren ads, which always signal important trends, you'll notice that the tendency to decorate with a southwestern theme has come and gone, unless you happen to have a ski condo in the Rockies or a summer place in Taos. Now all those ladies who had their decorators ripping out their crystal chandeliers and replacing them with silly looking arrangements of antlers holding tiny lights are taking aim at the antlers this time around.

The new trends are English colonial or French country. When you think of colonial, don't think Pilgrim forebears. Think, "the sun never sets on the British Empire"; think *Out of Africa*. And French country, folks, is more often than not French-Canadian country, because that's where a lot of the furniture in this style originated.

In fact, I've just learned that Canadian furniture, which was being trucked down into this country about ten years ago at a great rate, is now becoming more valuable in Canada, where people have decided they want it back. So Canadian dealers are coming to this country and paying more for it now than they sold it for a few years ago.

None of my observations are chiseled in stone, of course. The vast antiques and collectibles area is still unpredictable and chancy and that's half the fun. As you hunt for your favorite kind of treasure, the only thing you can really count on is that you're in for constant surprises.

The best surprise I found as I wandered around the country checking out the leads that turned into the information in this book, is that almost everyone

Some Things That Are Hot and Some That Are Not

HOT

Italian art glass. Everyone remembers this. People used to get these blown and shaped vases, bowls, etc., as wedding presents in the fifties, and almost everyone hated them. Not so now. Very good examples go for thousands.

Really old things. And by that we mean antiquities, like those Dr. Monroy sells in San Diego, rather than merely antiques. Surprisingly, a lot of ancient bric-a-brac isn't all that expensive. Remember, the more B.C. it is, the more P.C. it is.

Wrought iron. This favorite decorative medium of the sixties has had a huge revival. Actually, most of what you see is not truly wrought iron, worked and reworked by a blacksmith, but forged iron. How do you tell the difference? Wrought iron never rusts. There's lot of good old iron out there, and it's still relatively inexpensive; but keep in mind that a lot of the iron that came from Portugal in the sixties is what you're seeing now.

Dog paintings. If you didn't know that Americans love their pets, this ought to make it clear. Dog paintings, no matter what medium, age, size, frame, or condition, are so desirable that they disappear almost at once from any shop. The best, of course, are Victorian paintings or prints, often extremely sentimental in content. Watch out for fake prints; it's a little harder to create a fake oil inexpensively so many of these are okay, as long as they're cheap. If you looking at a lot of money, have an expert vet it for you.

Antique bed linens. These don't necessarily have to be linen; fine cotton is good, too. Especially popular are the large square pillow shams that are usually from Europe. Dealers now routinely travel through Ireland and parts of England buying up all of this they can find.

Flags. Because most people are patriotic enough to properly dispose of tattered and worn flags by carefully burning them, flags that depict the earlier conformation of the Union of States are hard to find, unless they've been stored in a cupboard somewhere. Mary Emmerling, who always knows, is big on flags, and that should tell you to snatch up every flag you can find—and rejoice if it turns out to have fewer than 50 stars. Also, any flag or banner associated with a military unit of any kind has extra value; get an expert to look at it.

Paisley shawls or throws. The intricately worked patterns of spirals and whorls would make it seem that paisley was produced in the Middle East, but in fact it was made in Europe, mostly in Scotland and France. Today, the best examples of paisley are in an Edinburgh paisley museum. Handworked is more valuable than machine-made but it can be difficult to tell the difference. If you can buy a shawl or throw for under $100, you've got a bargain.

NOT

Mirrored window frames. Probably because they're so useful in lighting up dark corners, these windows with mirror panes have been done to death. You can now buy them in most discount paint stores, which should tell you all you need to know. Still viable are mirrors in interesting and unusually shaped wood fragments—fans, portholes, arches.

Cows. Anything and everything cow-like, but especially those plywood cutout cows that people used to stand on their lawns. One important exception, Elsie, the Borden trademark cow. But be careful; Elsie's been brought back, so there are lots of new Elsie collectibles around. Outdated also applies to sheep and geese with or without bandannas.

Turquoise/silver jewelry. Because so much of it is made outside of this country, the appeal of this ethnic jewelry has faded. Really old Native American jewelry, often described as "old pawn" pieces, are still collectible, though.

Bird cages and bird houses. For a while there, every room layout in a shelter magazine came equipped with a vine-filled birdcage on a wall. If you're stuck with one and you don't actually want to fill it with a bird, put it outside in the garden, stand it on a tree stump, and fill it with perennials.

Fake old pine furniture. Everyone's seen the fat-legged coffee tables or harvest tables, the chests, bureaus, armoires, plate racks, sideboards or cupboards. However different the shape, the look is very distinctive—natural pine, covered with a coat or two of light brown Briwax. Sometimes the wood is even distressed a little to add authenticity. Look at the workmanship. Most of these repro pieces are a little sloppy—doors don't fit, drawers are loose, moldings don't match exactly. Look inside and underneath where the newness of the wood is always more obvious. Some are actually made from old pine boards, but you can still tell from the sharpness of the edges.

I met was willing to help me learn and add to my list of great places to explore, confirming my belief that when you go out after antiques, you are going to meet the nicest people in the world.

And, if you want to let me know where you found your favorite antique, or a really great place to check out, I'd love to hear from you. After all, my favorite antique, always, is just one shopping trip away from being found.

CHAPTER EIGHTEEN

PACIFIC COAST REGION

California, Oregon, Washington

CALIFORNIA

If there's one word to sum up the California antiques market, it's *eclectic*. On my first foray into a flea market here, I found a crossbow in working condition on one table next to a ceramic reclining naked lady who, on closer inspection, turned out to be a salt-and-pepper shaker set. Her bosoms, removable, were the shakers.

Glassware and pottery still appear in surprising amounts, in spite of earthquakes. California is a particularly good source for San Franciscan pottery; this firm went out of business a few years ago and as a result its patterns are now all collectibles. Furniture of any kind, from rustic to elegant, seems to be in short supply.

If you go to California, you can get the best view of the state's antiques resources by traveling all the way up the state from San Diego to the Oregon border on the Pacific Coast Highway, US Route 101. It is lined with dozens of antiques shops, most of them small, independent stores in charming little oceanside towns.

R.G. Canning Flea Markets

Most California dealers say they regularly cruise through these flea markets and use them as their primary sources for the stock they bring to their mall booths or shops.

The one considered to have the best variety and prices is the Rose Bowl Flea Market, conducted every second Sunday of the month at Rose Bowl stadium in Pasadena. Once a year, in the fall, the Rose Bowl market puts on an annual antiques and collectibles speak show that seems to be absolutely mandatory for the dealers out here. The Rose Bowl Sunday events open at 9:00 A.M. and cost $3.00 For early entry at 7 A.M, you pay double.

R. G. Canning also has a Ventura Flea Market in that oceanside city's Seaside Park. It is held every other month, on the third Sunday of the month, and most dealers seem to think it's almost as good as the Rose Bowl and sometimes even better. Because most of the merchandise is "smalls," the operative technique seems to be to bring along a laundry cart to hold all the goodies. One dealer in Ventura said she had seven spaces in different malls and filled them all with merchandise she finds in Ventura. Early entry at Ventura is $8, double the normal $4 admission. It's obvious the best buys are gone by the official opening time. We arrived at 9:00 A.M. exactly, and dealers had already filled trucks and were getting ready to drive away.

The city of Ventura also has an interesting downtown area a few blocks from the park that is filled with antiques shops of every stripe and variety, from exquisite and expensive showroom shops to consignment shops, flea markets, and thrift stores.

A third Canning flea market, in San Bernardino, is open every Sunday. The company also conducts special annual events in other towns in southern California.

FOR MORE INFORMATION: For a complete listing of all the R.G. Canning-sponsored antiques shows and flea market events, telephone 1-213-560-SHOW for a detailed recorded announcement. Real people only answer the phone on Mondays and Wednesdays.

Penny Pinchers

When a shop uses the word "junque" on a sign, I'm inclined to roll my eyes and pass it by, but Penny Pinchers, in the Simi Valley—the exurban valley beyond the more developed suburban San Fernando Valley on the outskirts of Los Angeles, is a delightful little mall, a real find.

This seventy-dealer, rambling store, located in a unprepossessing area in Simi, has some of the more interesting antiques I've seen in California.

The mall is owned and operated by Kathy Erwin and her son, Jim. She started it thirty years ago when it was, she says bluntly, "Just a junk shop, and not 'junque' either."

Now it has upgraded its merchandise and expanded into 17,000 square feet full of small items and furniture, too. There were some very unusual pieces—working traffic lights, fire memorabilia including brass hose handles, and rustic lodgepole furniture. It's worth noting, however, that when you're looking for antiques in California, a lot of the most authentic-looking pieces may not be deliberate fakes, but are not old. They were made at movie studios and used as props in films.

TO GET THERE: Take Interstates 405 or 5 north to the Highway 118 exit, turn west to Tapo Canyon St., then left on Cochran and right on Winifred to the dead end, which is Valley Fair.

FOR MORE INFORMATION: Write 4265 Valley Fair, Simi Valley, CA, 93065 or telephone 1-805-527-0056

Unicorn Antique Mall

This is where you get to meet Indiana Jones. Well, he may not be a movie star, but one of the dealers in the Unicorn Mall is Dr. Monroy, an actual working archeologist who goes out on digs in remote corners of the world, and what makes his booth so interesting are the treasures—little goddesses and things—that he brings back. He says he also buys from other dealers in antiquities.

Other dealers in this very pleasant, very affordably priced mall have everything from good Early American-quality furniture and glassware to fifties collectibles.

The mall is located in the Gas Lamp District in downtown San Diego, an area that used to be a slum but has gone through an extensive renovation to become a trendy collection of antiques shops, clothing boutiques, theaters, and restaurants.

Of all the area shops, Unicorn, with three floors in an old industrial building that covers an entire city block, seems to have the best supply.

TO GET THERE: Interstate 5 north or south, follow signs for downtown exits.

FOR MORE INFORMATION: Write to Unicorn Antique Mall, 704 J Street (corner 7th & J), San Diego, CA, 92101, or telephone 1-619-232-1696.

Cow Palace Antique Shows

Four times a year—February, May, August, and November—six hundred dealers assemble in San Francisco's Cow Palace for an antiques show that is always praised. The dealers, primarily from northern California, also come from farther north in Washington and Oregon. As a result, there are a fair number of Pacific Northwest Native American artifacts available at these shows, as well as many Asian antiques.

TO GET THERE: US Route 101 either south or north, get off at the Cow Palace Exit. The Cow Palace is located on Geneva Avenue.

FOR MORE INFORMATION: Palmer & Wirfs, 4001 NE Halsey, Portland, OR, 97232, or telephone 1-503-282-0877.

OREGON

Expo Center Antiques Show

In July close to seventeen hundred dealers converge on Portland, Oregon's Expo Center for the largest antiques show of the year. Dealers here come from every part of the country. Show owners Chris Palmer and Don Wirfs estimate that twenty-eight states are actually represented on the selling floor. Quality is good, and the Saturday and Sunday show seems to have a loyal following.

Palmer and Wirfs do two other Portland shows annually at the Expo Center; the other two, in March and October, are indoor shows and space is limited to the approximately twelve hundred indoor booths. The July show, however, includes all indoor booth spaces as well as another five hundred outdoors.

The shows are conducted on Saturdays and Sundays, with dealer setup on Friday. Early buying isn't really encouraged, but call for more information. Admission is $5 for the entire weekend.

TO GET THERE: The Expo Center is located at the north edge of the city at Exit 306B off Interstate 5, at 2060 North Marine Drive.

FOR MORE INFORMATION: Write to Palmer & Wirfs at 4001 Northeast Halsey, Portland, OR, 97232, or telephone 1-503-282-0877.

ADDENDUM: This firm also does a slightly smaller November antiques show at the Oregon Convention Center in Portland. The Conventions Center is newer, but only has space for 750 booths.

WASHINGTON

Pioneer Square Market

Seattle has a flourishing antiques district underground. The original buildings in the city's primary business area were all covered over back in the nineteenth century because flooding problems plagued them. New buildings were constructed on top of the old, and those hidden underneath the ground were either forgotten completely or occasionally used for storage.

Now the old buildings underneath the street level have been excavated, as have sidewalks and streets, and visitors can explore a past century by walking down into them. The Pioneer Square mall is at an adjacent level to the Old Town and has eighty dealers with some very unusual and interesting antiques in 11,000 square feet.

There's a second underground antiques mall, the Seattle Underground Mall, a block away. Three blocks farther south on Jackson Street, still in the twenty-square-block Pioneer Square area, are two more malls.

On the waterfront, which has undergone extensive renovation, is a large new mall, the Downtown Antiques Market. It is close to the Pike Place Market, the huge multishop facility that replaced a derelict port factory.

The two most unique malls in the area are the Old Firehouse Antiques Mall on Alaska Way, and the Antiques Emporium, a longtime Seattle antiques shop crammed with really good finds. The Antiques Emporium had a fire last year but has rebuilt and reopened.

TO GET THERE: Interstate 5 to the center of the city, follow Pioneer Square signs.

FOR MORE INFORMATION: Pioneer Square Antique Mall, 1-206-624-1164.

ADDENDUM: The East Side of Puget Sound in Washington was originally expected to become the capital of the state. Many luxurious mansions were built in this area in expectation of strong economic development here. When that failed to happen, many of these old homes fell into disrepair. Now, many are being bought up and restored, but the Port Townsend and Port Angeles areas still have a lot of interesting antiques that came out of these houses.

Star Center Mall

This 175-dealer mall in Snohomish, a small town about forty-five minutes northeast of Seattle, has a reputation as one of the most well-run malls in the Pacific Northwest. Dealers show on five different levels and the mall is open seven days a week.

Merchandise runs the gamut from locally acquired estate sale antiques to pieces brought from Brimfield.

The same firm operates three other slightly smaller malls, located in Centralia, Washington (Centralia Square); Lafayette, Oregon (Lafayette Schoolhouse Mall); and Seaside, Oregon (Seaside Mall).

TO GET THERE: From Seattle, take Interstate 405 north to Route 9, which goes into Snohomish. The mall is at the intersection of Second and Union.

FOR MORE INFORMATION: Write to 829 Second St., Snohomish, WA 98290 or telephone 1-360-568-2131.

CHAPTER NINETEEN

RESOURCES

All too often, the one thing that stops a beautiful piece from reaching perfection is a small but vital element—the glass ball that fits into a brass turkey claw leg on a piano stool, or the broken runner that has immobilized an otherwise beautiful eighteenth-century rocking chair.

Fortunately, there are a lot of people and places out there willing to offer remedies for virtually every kind of replacement and repair problem. Here are some of the best.

The two best catalogs I've found for every kind of general need are:

Constantine's
2050 Eastchester Road
Bronx, NY 10461

1-718-792-1600
Toll Free: 1-800-223-8087
Fax Free: 1-800-225-WOOD
Catalogue: Free

Constantine's has almost everything you could ever need to work with wood, either by refinishing and repairing or building from scratch. This catalog is especially useful if you're going to want to replace inlay or veneer.

Van Dyke's Restorers
P.O. Box 278
Woonsocket, SD 57385
Toll Free: 1-800-843-3320
FAX: 1-605-796-4085

This catalog is my personal favorite, because there are so many interesting and unusual things in it. This is where you find those glass balls for a turkey claw leg, or the curved glass you might need to replace a broken glass door in an old secretary desk. You can get a replacement roll top for a desk, or a curved Queen Ann Leg for a table, caning supplies, hardware . . . it goes on and on. If you buy shaped glass in their standard sizes, it's surprisingly inexpensive. I replaced a door for about $40. Shipping was prompt and also inexpensive and the glass arrived in one piece.

Ordering is easy; everyone seems courteous and attentive.

Other Good Resources:

Specialty Hardware:

If your antique bureau is missing a drawer pull, Winston Harness will hand cast a duplicate for you if you send him an original to copy. Prices are extremely reasonable for custom work—$15 for a simple ring pull up to $35 or $45 for a more complicated design. He reproduces other types of hardware as well. It usually takes him about three weeks to complete an order.

Winston Harness
501 North Sixth Street
DeSota, MO, 63020
1-314-337-5693
or e-mail to http://OURWORLD.com/HomePages/
BRNZCASTER

Machine Made Hardware:

Horton Brasses, Inc.
Nooks Hill Road, P.O. Box 95
Cromwell, CT, 06416
1-860-635-4450
Fax:1-860-635-6473

Horton is one of the most respected names in the replacement hardware world. They offer authentic reproductions of brass and wooden drawer pulls and other specialty hardware, as well as porcelain knobs, clock parts, and mirror hardware. How-to videos also available.

Grandpa Snazzy's Hardware
1832 So. Broadway
Denver, CO, 80210
1-303-778-6508
Fax: 1-303-733-2323

This small store in the heart of Denver's antique district stocks original and replacement hardware, including those wonderful old glass kitchen door pulls, and some of the most elaborate door knobs I've ever seen. It's an exceptionally good place to call if you're not sure exactly what you need. Fax them a sketch or photo of the piece you have to fix up, and they'll choose the right drawer pulls or hardware for you. They're always right, too. No catalog, because their stock of original hardware changes constantly, but telephone and fax consultations make ordering easy.

Wrought-Iron Hardware, Foundry:

Kayne & Son Hardware
76 Daniel Ridge Rd.
Candler, NC, 28715

1-704-667-8868
Fax: 1-704-665-8303

This is the place to go for wrought-iron replacements. The firm has a foundry and can cast metal. The firm will reproduce anything from a small part of a hinge to a large item. There is a catalog available of designs if you don't know exactly what it is you need. So if you have a broken bronze sculpture—a tail off a horse or arm off of a statue—they can mend it for you.

Basket and Caning Supplies:

H. H. Perkins Company
10 So. Bradley Road
Woodbridge, CT, 06525
1-203-389-9501
1-800-462-6600

A reliable source of caning supplies, tools, and other materials relating to the restoration and repair of antiques. Dealers use this firm frequently.

Cane & Basket Supply Company
1283 So. Cochran
Los Angeles, CA, 90019
1-213-939-9644
1-800-468-3966

Extensive basketry, hand caning, and machine caning supplies as well as lots of seating materials— pressed fiber replacement seats, rawhide stripping, Shaker tape, and even supplies to replace Danish modern chair webbing and cushion supports.

Gingerbread trims, Victorian:

Vintage Woodworks
Hwy. 34 South, P.O. Box R
Quinlan, TX, 75474
1-903-356-2158
Fax: 1-903-356-3023

You've probably seen ads for this company in the backs of magazines. In addition to extensive woodworking supplies and trim for restoring old houses, this firm also stocks gazebos, folding screens, screen replacement parts, shelving, and gallery rails. Very useful catalog.

Lighting Supplies:

B & P Lamp Supply
843 Old Morrison Hwy.
McMinnville, TN, 37110
1-615-473-3016
Fax: 1-615-473-3014

This is a wholesale-only source for replacement parts for antique lighting fixtures as well as some very authentic-looking reproduction kerosene lamps and shades. Get a friendly dealer to help you get a catalog because their glass shade selection is so very good—everything from those painted *Gone with the Wind* globes and chandelier shades in a wide selection of designs, to replacement torchere shades and Aladdin lamp parts.

Lighting—Early American:

Authentic Designs
29 The Mill Road
West Rupert, VT, 05776
1-802-394-7713

The lanterns, chandeliers, and wall sconces available here are all custom-crafted re-creations of traditional colonial and Early American designs in authentic materials such as maple, copper, brass, copper terne, and tin. Everything is handcrafted using exactly the same methods early artisans used to create the original fixtures.

Locks:

The Wise Company
P.O. Box 118
Arabi, LA, 70032
1-504-277-7551

Colonial Lock Company
172 Main Street
Terryville, CT, 06786
1-203-584-0311

Small Good Things:

MILK PAINT:

The Old Fashioned Milk Paint Company
P.O. Box 222
Groton, MA, 01450
1-617-448-6336

NAILS, SQUARE:
Tremont Nail Company
Box 111
Wareham, MA, 02571
1-508-295-0038

PORCELAIN CASTERS (FOR VICTORIAN FURNITURE):
Ritter & Son Hardware
P.O. Box 578
Gualala, CA, 95445
1-800-358-9120

SHAKER SEAT TAPES AND SUPPLIES:
Shaker Workshops
P.O. Box 1028
Concord, MA, 01742
1-617-646-8985

RESOURCES

TACKS, DECORATIVE:
Turner & Seymour
P.O. Box 358
Torrington, CT, 06790
1-203-489-9214

TIN, PIERCED:
Country Accents
R.D. 2, P.O. Box 293
1-201-996-2885

TRUNK SUPPLIES:
Charlotte Ford Trunks
P.O. Box 536
Spearman, TX, 79081
1-806-659-3027

VICTORIAN WALLPAPER:
Victorian Collectibles Ltd.
845 Glenbrook Rd.
Milwaukee, WI, 53217
1-414-352-6910

Victorian Lampshade Frames:

ARO Wire Products, Inc.
2122 Aaron Street
Los Angeles, CA 90025
Tel: 213-36-89-2391

Large selection of unusual and elaborate shapes
reasonably priced

Mitchell's Shady Business

2724 Austin Drive
Mesquite, TX 75181
Tel: 1-972-222-0764

Frames can be purchased unfinished or finished with beads and fringe.

Museum conservation catalogs:

Conservation Materials
240 Freeport Boulevard
Box 2889
Sparks, NV
Telephone: 1-702-331-0582

University Products, Inc.
So. Canal Street
Holyoke, MA 01040
Tel:1-800-628-1912

Custom made wire lampshades:

Also eighty-five to ninety other designs in catalog. Catalho, $3, refundable on first order:

Victorian Wire Design
P.O. Box 220303
Milwaukee, Oregon 97269-0303

Silver restoring and replating:

Also copper, brass, and pewter.

New England Country Silver, Inc.
25 Smith Rd, P.O. Box 271
East Haddam, CT 06423
1-860-873-1314

CHAPTER TWENTY

PUBLICATIONS

There are two reference books that no antiques enthusiast should be without. They are, in order of importance:

The Furniture Doctor by George Grotz
(Doubleday, 1989, $14.95)
Grotz' book is an invaluable guide to recognizing furniture and figuring out how to repair it. Most dealers I know own a copy or have at least read this book. It's considered within the trade to be a valuable standard reference work.

The Readers' Digest Fix-It Manual
(Readers' Digest Books)
This book has extremely helpful how-to chapters on repair techniques that almost anyone can master.

There are instructions for repairing everything from the springs in a piece of upholstered furniture to replacing hinges on a drop-leaf table. The directions on how to cane by hand, as well as how to install machine caning, are the best I've ever found.

Trade Publications:

There are a lot of antiques newspapers that appear regionally throughout the country, and offer everything from articles on aspects of the trade to classified ads and auction notices. Of these, two are exceptional, and are read by dealers and collectors around the country because the information they impart is so valuable.

They are:

The Maine Antique Digest
P.O. Box 1429
Waldboro, ME, 04572
1-207-832-4888

Published monthly, at $29 for an annual subscription, this newspaper is the biggest antiques bargain in the country. The paper comes in at least seven, and often more, fat sections and is chock-full of articles that can be on everything from investigative reports to historical research. I've never picked up an issue that didn't have something in it that I wanted to save. There's always lots of auction news, with prices. That's valuable because it's a good way to see which way the market winds are blowing. Show notices and display and classified ads are also included.

Antiques and the Arts Weekly
Bee Publishing Company
5 Church Hill Road
Newtown Connecticut 08470
1-203-426-3141

A weekly publication known in the trade more familiarly as the *Newtown Bee,* this newspaper ranks next to its sister publication in Maine in terms of content. Essentially the same format, but fewer prices seem to appear. An annual subscription costs $38.

Regionally:

These are just a few of the area publications available. Although they are all distributed free in participating antiques shops, shows, and malls, most are also available by subscription if you don't mind paying for it. Subscriptions are especially useful if you're looking for a specific collectible or antique category, or if you plan to visit a different part of the country and want to do a little advance planning. Most will probably send you a sample copy free of charge.

Antique Almanac
The New York Eye Publishing Co., Inc.
P.O. Box 2400
New York, NY, 10021

(A smallish newspaper with emphasis on New York State and environs. Subscription, $10 per year for twelve issues, or $1.50 each.)

Antique & Collectibles
Box 1565
El Cajon, CA 92022
(Features news and articles about California events, and some in neighboring Arizona.)

Antique Review
12 East Stafford Avenue
Worthington, OH, 43085
(Features the midwestern states. Very informative, lots of sections, conscientious writing.)

The Antique Shopper
37600 Hills Tech Drive
Farmington Hills, MI, 48331
(A small midwestern publication with auction and show news. $19 for twelve issues.)

Antique Trader
P.O. Box 1050
Dubuque, IA, 52004-1050
(A very large circulation, weekly midwestern publication that continues to grow in size. Includes useful columns as well as show, auction, club, and dealer news. One-year subscription, $35 for 52 weekly issues.)

Antiques Gazette
P.O. Box 305
Hammond, LA 70404
1-504-429-0575.
Covers the South from Florida to Houston. Published monthly, $14 for 12 issues.

The Antiques Journal
P.O. Box 120
Ware, MA, 01082
(Well-written, heavily illustrated, and features the entire Northeastern U.S. Subscription, $12 per year for twelve issues.)

Brimfield Antique Guide
P.O. 442
Brimfield, MA, 01010
(Printed three times a year, this publication is distributed free at all the Brimfield shows. It includes advertising for upcoming events far and wide. A one-year subscription is $11.95. Especially useful if you're going to Brimfield for the first time or want to show at one of the markets.)

County Lines
P.O. Box 31
Westown, PA, 19395
(Monthly magazine featuring dining, shopping, and show information within the southeastern Pennsylvania and northern Delaware area. Twelve issues for $29.)

The Country Register
6055 East Lake Mead Blvd.
#A164
Las Vegas, NV, 89115-6909

(Covers Nevada, and is published every two months. Subscription, $12 per year.)

Fence Posts
421 Main St.
Windsor, LA 80550
1-800-275-5646
(Published weekly; $27.00 per year.)
(Not really an antiques publication, this small, western-focus magazine is worth it because it features a lot of western and midwestern farm and ranch auctions not normally listed in antiques guides.)

Flea Market Shoppers Guide
P.O. Box 8
LaHabra, CA 90633-0008
(Distributed free at all the California flea market events run by R.G. Canning Enterprises. The articles aren't much, but the ads are very worthwhile reading.)

The Hudson Valley Antiquer
P.O. Box 640
Rhinebeck, NY 12571
One year subscription, $18.95
(Serves the Hudson River Valley area in upstate New York. Also available, the *Western Connecticut/ Massachusetts Antiquer*.)

PUBLICATIONS

MassBay Antiques
Community Newspaper Company
2 Washington Street, P.O. Box 192
Ipswich, MA, 01938
(Very readable publication serving Massachusetts, including Cape Cod, as well as Rhode Island and Connecticut. A one-year subscription costs $15.)

New Century Collector
P.O. Box 510432
Salt Lake City, Utah 84151

Today's Collector
700 East State Street
Iola, WI, 54990-0001
(Twelve issues of this glossy newsmagazine that covers the entire United States are available for a special price of $17.95. Lots of news and resources; a very good buy.)

Treasure Chest
Treasure Chest Publishing, Inc.
Box 245
North Scituate, RI 02847-0245

Unravel the Gavel
P.O. Box 171
Ctr. Barnstead, NH, 03225
(Auction news in the Northeast, plus articles and ads. Subscription rates are $10 for six issues, $15 for twelve if sent bulk rate, and $25 for twelve issues sent first-class.)

INDEX

Internet (*continued*)
  verification of authentic-
    ity, 101
  See also Web, World
    Wide (WWW)
Iowa:
  AmVet Charity Antiques
    Show, 142
  Banowetz Antique Malls,
    142–43
  Christmas Walk, 142
  McGregor, 143–44
  Walnut, 141–42
Ivory objects, 89–90, 183

Jewelry, 221
  costume, 137, 140, 237
  estate, 28, 31, 223, 237
  Hyde Park Antiques Cen-
    ter (NY), 65
  Native American, 103,
    226, 242
  Tepper Galleries (NY),
    60
  turquoise, 139, 242
  See also Metal objects

Kansas:
  additional sites, 145
  Wichita Mid-America
    Flea Market, 144–45
Kentucky:
  450–mile yard sale, 7,
    109–12
  Lexington Summer An-
    tique & Collectibles
    Show, 113
  Louisville, 112

Kitchen collectibles, 140
  reproductions of, 128
  serving pieces, 190–91
  white ironstone china,
    8–9

Lamps, 27
  experts on, 221–22
  kerosene lanterns, 131,
    192
  supplies for, 263–64
  Tepper Galleries (NY),
    60
  Tiffany-style, 51
  See also Lighting fixtures
Leather, restoration of, 161
Lighting fixtures, 23, 94,
    172
  chandeliers, 67
  Lampshade Shop (ME),
    23
  reproductions, 261
  supplies for, 260–61
  See also Lamps
Louisiana:
  Fireside Antiques, 117
  Magazine Street, 118
  Ponchatoula, 118

Maine:
  Arundel Antiques, 25
  Bridgton Main Street
    shops, 23–24
  Montsweag Flea Market,
    25–26
  Naples shops, 23
  Wales & Hamblen, 23

Museums:
  Armory Museum (CO),
    196
  computer access to, 100
  for research, 134–35, 188

National Register of His-
    toric Landmarks, 149
Native American items:
  beadwork, 103
  Coeur d'Alene (ID), 201
  grindstones, 78
  jewelry, 103, 139
  moccasins, 206
  Pacific Northwest, 250
  rightful ownership of,
    226
  Rubber Snake Ranch
    (WY), 198
  Wyoming, Web site, 103
Nebraska, Buffalo County
    Antique Flea Market,
    147–48
Needlework:
  embroidery, 8, 51, 234
  hooked rugs, 234
  paisley shawls/throws,
    241
  quilts, 128, 132–33,
    154–56
  See also Fabric
Nevada, Las Vegas Malls:
  Antique Sampler, 222–23
  Gypsy Caravan, 223
  Red Rooster, 221–22
New Century Collector, 220
New Hampshire:
  Antique Alley, 29

Burlwood Antique Cen-
    ter, 31
Colonial Plaza Antique
    Markets, 30
Lake Winnipesaukee An-
    tique District, 31–32
Prospect Hill Antiques,
    30–31
New Jersey:
  Atlantique City show, 58
  Golden Nugget Antique
    Market, 55–56
  Lambertville Antique
    Market, 55–56
  Mullica Hill, 57–58
New Mexico, 225–28
  El Collectivo Antiques
    Market, 227
  Indian Market, 227, 228
  Sweenie Center, 227
New York:
  Copake Country Auc-
    tion, 63
  East Hampton dump, 7,
    10
  Eastern Long Island,
    65–66
  Hudson, 66
  Hudson Valley, 62
  Hyde Park Antiques Cen-
    ter, 64
  Long Island, vii
  Madison-Bouckville An-
    tiques Show, 61–62
  Rhinebeck Antiques
    Fair, 63–64
  Tepper Galleries, 60–61
  Twenty-sixth Street &

Primitives:
Billings (MT), 200
Centreville (MI), 174–75
furniture, 97, 113, 170, 195
Hillsville (VA), 96
Kearney (NE), 148
Laurel (DE), 71
McGregor (IA), 143
restoration of, 153
Round Top Roundup (TX), 228
See also Native American items
Provenance, 127, 133, 211, 226
Publications list, 267–73

Railroad memorabilia, 201
Reference books, 100
See also Price guides
Renninger's Antique Guide, 52
Repairs. *See* Restoration
Reproductions:
furniture, 129, 242
vs. genuine, 60, 125–40, 196–97
glassware, 89, 126–27, 136
lighting fixtures, 261
movie studio, 248
small items, 219
toys, 125–26, 129
Restoration, 151–65
fixer-uppers, where to purchase, 18, 92, 177
parts, locating, xvi, 101

resources, 255–65
Rhode Island:
Blue Flag Antiques, 22–23
Buck's Unlimited, 19–20
General Stanton Flea Market, 20–22
Little Compton Antiques Show, 22
Tiverton's Four Corners area, 22

Salt-and-pepper shakers, 130
Selling your own antiques, 203–16
Shills, 39–40, 132
Ship models, 139
Shops, antiques, 78, 85–86, 103
Shows, antiques, 78, 84–86, 108
Signs:
advertising, 190, 194
decorative, 140
Silver, 65, 88–89, 186
Sleighs, 26–27
Small items, 27, 246–47
Bridgton (ME), 23
McGregor (IA), 144
Quechee (VT), 27
Wells (ME), 24
See also Decorative accessories; Glassware; Lamps
South Carolina, 93–96
Antiques for the Home Show, 94–95